Beat
the
Casino

Beat the Casino

Frank Barstow

POCKET BOOKS

New York   London   Toronto   Sydney   Tokyo

The data and opinions contained herein have been carefully prepared and assembled. They, however, cannot be guaranteed. The publisher and the author specifically disclaim any intent to induce readers to gamble or to assure them of a favorable outcome should they do so.

POCKET BOOKS, a division of Simon & Schuster Inc.
1230 Avenue of the Americas, New York, N.Y. 10020

ISBN: 0-671-67427-7

First Pocket Books printing January 1986

10   9   8   7   6   5   4   3

POCKET and colophon are trademarks of Simon & Schuster Inc.

Printed in the U.S.A.

To Marianne, a fine and courageous lady who had no taste for gambling. Without her encouragement, enthusiasm, and unflagging interest, this project might never have been undertaken, let alone completed.

Acknowledgment

I am grateful to Major Riddle of the Dunes Hotel, whose *Weekend Gamblers Handbook* in the early '60s stimulated my interest in casino games. Also to Allan Wilson, Scarne, Roberts, Revere, O'Neil-Dunne, and the others whose writings and opinions are mentioned in this text. Special thanks also to June Shields who frequently came to the rescue with appropriate ideas or phrases when my mind seemed to black out, probably due to three-finger typophobia. I am also indebted to Stan Roberts, the well-known blackjack expert, for reviewing my page proofs. Some of the changes he suggested are incorporated in the book's strategy tables for that popular game.

F.B.

Table of Contents

List of Tables

List of Systems

Primary descriptive pages only

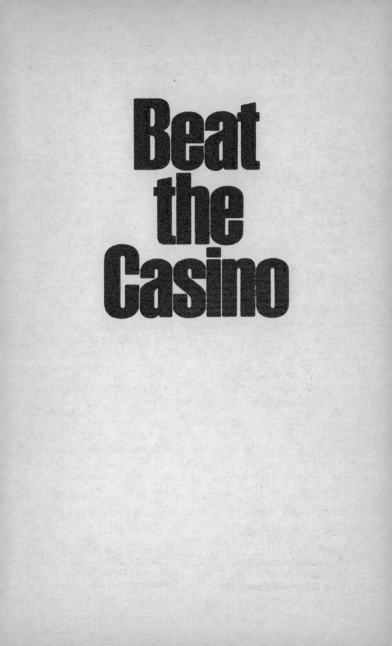

Beat the Casino

Introduction

I f you toss a coin 100 times, you can expect a series of 6 or more successive heads or tails at least once, 5 or more at least three times, 4 or more six times, 3 or more 14 times, and 2 or more 33 times. These figures are based on the laws of probability and the theory of permutations and combinations. Devotees of games of chance must often wonder if there were not some practical means by which they could latch on to these repeat sequences of even chances — and cash in on them. Well, they can — and several practical solutions to the problem are embodied in systems you are about to meet.

If anyone had told me a few years ago that I might one day write a book on gambling systems, my response would have been that he was dreaming. What could be more farfetched than a man reared in the most conservative bastions of Wall Street authoring a book telling people how to shoot craps?

I gravitated into Wall Street right after college and had my original training with one of the most conservative of the major financial institutions in this country. The "prudent man" approach was the only one we believed in; there was no such thing as a "safe security," etc. Yet our functioning was always directly or indirectly tied in with the gyrations of what many regard as the world's greatest gambling institution, the New York Stock Exchange.

As an investment banking executive and stockbroker with several of the largest and most prestigious firms in the United States over a 40-year span, I've had a voice in many multimillion dollar decisions. I've learned to hedge my bets when possible, to think independently, and, quite often, contrarily. Crowd thinking is so often wrong.

When the stakes are high and the risk great, you take insurance if you can get it. Before you sign on the dotted line, you consult major clients to secure advance commitments, and then you form a syndicate to spread the risk.

Of course, when you gamble in a casino there are no clients to consult, but you can hedge your bets. You can have a partner who has to win if you lose. You can combine two systems that usually offset each other, though both can, and often do, win at the same time. By such tactics one can, at the very least, slow his rate of loss, thus buying time that should enable him to stay in the game until his luck turns.

Widely accepted concepts are often wrong. The books say there's no such thing as a winning system. Yet there are a few individuals — very few — who make their living at dice and 21, and they all use systems. I have been a winner at craps for the past three years and before that I'd been a winner at blackjack for many years — and I am definitely a system player.

The books also tell you that the best way to win at craps is to bet pass, come, and take the odds, which of course is a system. They also advise you never to run out on luck; let it run out on you. The fact is, however, if you always quit while winning, you'll do far better than if you wait for your luck to turn.

In many of the systems described in these pages, you will discern the influence of my earlier years. My rejection of certain beliefs widely held in gambling circles, my partiality toward hedged bets and the partnership concept — all these things reflect that influence. Nevertheless, I assure you that several of the systems I like and recommend can, and often do, produce profit fast enough to suit any taste, however demanding.

The sole objective of this book is to add to your enjoyment while playing casino craps, roulette, blackjack (21), or baccarat,* by showing you how to improve your chances of

---

*Baccarat is the only casino game in which a single bet (banker) wins more than 50 percent of the time. It is, therefore, an ideal vehicle for system players and for betting systems designed for opposing nearly-even chances. Although this game is not specifically covered in *Beat The Casino*, baccarat players will find that more than half the book's recommended systems are readily adaptable to their favorite game.

winning. In any endeavor, whether it be business, contract bridge, sex, tennis, or gambling, one's enjoyment tends to vary directly with his skill and understanding.

There are many books dealing with casino games, and some of them are excellent and comprehensive in their coverage — until they come to the vital matter of how to win or hold one's own in the games of pure chance such as craps and roulette. In those games, knowledge of the odds is important, but the controlling factor in winning or losing is almost always money management, which is just another name for betting systems. The systems that one finds written up fall generally into one of three categories: (1) the popular and conventional systems that have been supporting casinos for years; (2) novel systems that are sure to lose; and (3) novel systems calling for excessive risk taking relative to possible profit.

Within these pages you will find systems in the first category above clearly labeled as such — but you will also find a great many innovative and practical systems, some of which are original and most of which, to the best of my knowledge, have never before been published. You will also find clear enough expositions of the three major casino games to enable you to play skillfully and comfortably even on your first attempt.

The paucity of reliable published data on sensible betting systems probably reflects blind acceptance by mathematicians, physicists, and others of one highly questionable premise. The oft-repeated assertion that in the long run no system can ever overcome unfair odds has come to be accepted as fact. Indeed, it is fact if we interpret "long run" as implying that the system must be adhered to, no matter where it leads us. Any system will fail at some point if it is followed to the bitter end regardless of cost. However, if "long run" may just as well be construed to mean an endless series of short runs, then I believe the premise to be false.

In a contest between a player and a casino under existing rules, given approximately equal resources and a two percent or less house advantage, I am convinced that the player with a really good system would have a distinct edge. As a matter of fact, you will be introduced to several systems which, on the basis of extensive tests, appear to swing the odds or percentages over to the player's side, regardless of the disparity between his financial resources and the casino's.

Characteristic of virtually all published material on games of chance are phrases like "the gambler's fallacy" and "the gambler's ruin," or (as indicated above), "In the long run it is impossible for any system to overcome a percentage that favors the house!" That percentage is often referred to as the player's "minus expectancy."

The gambler's fallacy is his conviction that an abnormal sequence of occurrences is likely to end in accordance with the laws of probability, and at just about the time he decides to bet that it will end. His "ruin," of course, is what happens to him on that fateful day when the laws of chance appear to have been suspended and the 100 to 1 or 1000 to 1 event actually happens.

A puzzling aspect of nearly all analyses of progressive betting systems is the unvarying assumption that the system player pursues his system to the bitter end — and so ultimately must meet disaster. I find it impossible to imagine any intelligent person raising or doubling his wagers to a point where he's risking something like $500 in order to win $1. Yet that is the sort of premise upon which systems, per se, are generally dismissed as being useless.

In his erudite treatise, "The Casino Gambler's Guide," Allan Wilson, the well-known author and physicist, refers to a particularly "intriguing" procedure which he calls "Oscar's System." He says the inventor made scores or hundreds of trips from Southern California to Las Vegas, always covering his expenses by playing this progressive system with a profit objective of $1 each time he started a new series. Wilson ran a computer test of the system, which indicated the odds that the player would win his $1 before he ran into the house limit of $500 were 4,250 to 1. He then calculated that even if the odds had been 5,000 to 1, the player would have had no better than a 37 percent chance of 50 successful weekends with no losses; the same 37 percent chance of 50 weekends with just one loss; and an 18 percent chance of two "ruinous" losses. To drive home his point that even good systems are bad, Wilson estimated that each time the player reached the house $500 betting limit, his loss to that point would have approximated $13,000 — while the poor guy was playing to win exactly $1.

I was not overly impressed with Oscar's System as described, but I would bet my eye teeth that to win his $1, Oscar never ventured a wager in excess of $30, if that much. My point is simply that if one uses a faulty premise, he must inevitably reach a faulty conclusion.

There are, in fact, scores of progressive betting systems for even chances that do make mathematical sense, but every one of them must have a cut-off point that bears a reasonable relation to the risk-reward factor. Even the simple Martingale (1-2-4-8, etc.) has value as a tool in the gambler's arsenal when used intelligently. For example, tests of over 7,000 dice decisions showed that whenever they first alternated from pass to don't pass or vice versa, there was a 10 or 11 to 1 probability that one of the next three decisions also would be a reversal. That being so, a bet series of 1-2-4 on the three following decisions would prove a consistent winner on balance, even though the bettor would have to accept many losses of 7 units each.

All the progressive-type systems in this book have cut-off points, and they are all realistic relative to risk and profit potential. *Moreover, I am satisfied that no less than three of these hitherto unpublished systems, when properly played by two partners, or one person playing as if he were a two-man team, actually reverse the percentages, putting them on the players' side rather than the casino's.* Of course, this statement will be challenged, but my answer is that there's no substitute for experience. These systems have been thoroughly tested on paper and in the casinos.

This may be the first published work advocating some systems in which bets are increased as one loses. Most authorities insist that this tactic is unsound; that it is "sending good money after bad," and that the only time to raise bets is when the money risked wasn't the bettor's to begin with. When you do escalate your bets, they tell you to do so as rapidly as possible because if you don't, that old bugaboo, the player's "minus expectancy," is sure to catch up with you. Winning streaks don't last forever, so when you're in one, they insist that the way to capitalize on it is to jump your bets as rapidly as possible, as long as it is "their" money, not yours, that you're risking.

Although it is really your money, not "theirs," this conventional thinking has some merit, but it is unsound in several respects. My main argument with it is not that its concept is entirely erroneous, but that its claim to exclusivity as the only way to gamble intelligently simply does not stand up.

The up-as-you-lose approach has certain obvious attributes. It is the surest way to win if, without any intervening runs of extraordinary luck, one loses well over half his bets. It is also the surest way to overcome an earlier loss, and the laws of probability are almost always on the bettor's side. One should never lose sight of the fact that it is as difficult to guess wrong on an even proposition five or six times in a row as it is to guess right that many times.

The disadvantages of this approach are too well documented to need further exposition here. Suffice it to say that there are money-management systems that win with a 45 percent batting average — and without inordinate risk. If that were not so, I might be an unenthusiastic subscriber to the conventional viewpoint — but it is so.

The chief requirements are (1) that maximum risk in a single series of bets be limited to a fraction (generally one-third or less) of one's stake; (2) that profit potential in terms of dollars and the time factor bear a respectable relation to risk; and (3) that the normal win-lose ratio based on extensive testing prove adequate to more than offset the losses that are bound to occur from time to time. You will find that each such system specifically endorsed by me meets these requirements.

Over the years there have been so many promotions of

worthless systems for "beating" the various games of chance that claims of that nature are customarily and properly greeted with healthy skepticism. Regarding my own statements and claims, "Let me make this perfectly clear."

No system in this book is represented to be a "sure thing." However, I firmly believe that with skillful handling, quite a few of them will win fairly consistently, as well as on balance. As to those systems for which I've suggested partnership play, I hesitate to use the term "foolproof," but several of them very nearly merit that description. Of course, the partners have to execute their assignments correctly and with some judgment.

What do I mean by "skillful handling"? Some of the answers are: (1) quitting at the right time; (2) adjusting or changing bet selection methods and/or betting systems so as to respond to conditions of the moment; (3) raising and lowering bet levels as the circumstances warrant; (4) avoiding stubborn persistence in a losing cause and/or pressing a good winning streak until all profit has evaporated; (5) changing tables freely. These are a few of the things that can spell the difference between success and failure at the tables.

This book is the product of a lifetime of dealing with figures and probabilities in the fields of corporate finance and securities analysis and of 3,000 hours of actual casino play experimenting with every viable system that could be applied to craps, roulette, and blackjack — plus an additional 2,000 hours of analyzing and testing systems in my gambling workshop against my records of thousands of casino decisions.

Since retirement five years ago I have made perhaps 200 visits to casinos and clubs in Nevada, San Juan, Nassau, and London — and I've tried conscientiously to incorporate in these pages the essence of just about everything useful that my experiences have taught me.

If the data in this book helps you to win enough to cover the costs of your visits to resort areas around the world or to avoid losses that could have inhibited the pleasure of those visits, I shall feel well rewarded for the time and effort that have gone into its preparation.

CHAPTER 1

Some Basic Misconceptions

The major reason for the profitability of gambling establishments is what is called the "house percentage." This percentage is the product of an immutable mathematical law which, simply put, says that the long-range results of chance happenings are predetermined by the number of circumstances which will produce those happenings as opposed to the number of like circumstances which will prevent them. In the case of every bet* covered by a casino, there are more ways for the casino to win than there are for it to lose.

Accordingly, mathematics pundits have always insisted — at least for public consumption — that there was no way for the player to overcome what they called his "minus" or "negative" expectancy; that in the long run he had to lose. I disagree. In fact, I disagree with many of the old clichés which have been drummed into the public's consciousness so incessantly that their acceptance as fact is just about universal.

In this chapter I shall show you that:

1. The gambler's minus expectancy *can* be overcome.
2. Increasing bets as one loses is not necessarily foolish; on the contrary, it is probably the surest way to win.
3. System players do *not* always lose; quite the contrary.
4. Although dice and roulette wheels have no memories, the chance of an occurrence repeating itself does *not* remain constant regardless of the number of times it has already repeated.

---

*The payment by casinos of correct odds on "line" bets in craps, merely reduces the house percentage on the complete bets, including the odds.

5. The so-called "house percentage" does not reflect the true odds against the player.
6. The person with $50 of risk money or less should not confine his gambling to slot machines, Keno, and odd-ball mechanical games.

THE NEGATIVE EXPECTANCY

The premise that the player's minus expectancy in all casino games must catch up with him in the long run, is based on infinity. As a practical matter, however, gambling is done over periods of minutes, hours, and days. Our concern, therefore, is with mathematical probabilities or certainties within reasonable periods of time.

The laws of probability tell us that the percentage differential between two equal chance happenings must narrow as the number of chances is increased. We know that even though the chances may be equal, they are not likely to occur alternately except in short sequences. The theory of permutations and combinations teaches that their occurrences will conform roughly to certain patterns; that heads and tails, red and black, pass and don't pass will all have repeat runs as well as alternating runs of varying length, and that the longer the run, the less frequent its occurrence will be. Incidentally, these repeat and alternating sequences often play a major role in defeating the player's minus expectancy.

A Foolproof System: Suppose we're at the crap table betting pass. We will bet $1 to start and raise our bet $1 after each decision, win or lose, continuing to bet pass until we are ahead. If passes and misses are about evenly divided, we know we'll soon have a profit, but let's see what might happen if we get off to a bad start with misses heavily predominant.

I went over some two or three thousand Las Vegas dice decisions looking for the greatest disparity between passes and don'ts that I could find. In the most extreme case there were only four passes in the first 27 decisions. Continuing in that same session, the numbers became 17 vs. 33 and then 32 vs. 50, all, of course, in favor of don't pass. If you had been betting pass and using this 1 2 3 4 5 system, here is how your results would have appeared at these several stages:

Pass vs. Don't	4 vs. 23	17 vs. 33	32 vs. 50
$s Won vs. $s Lost	82 vs. 296	*591 vs. 682	1637 vs. 1763

About 70 decisions beyond the point at which I stopped scoring, I noticed 11 almost-consecutive passes — only one don't pass in the middle. At that point each win would have been worth almost $160 and our pass bettor surely would have emerged victorious. Even though he had to invest $13,000 or so in order to win, I trust I have made my point. In 500 or 1,000 bets on any even proposition, using a simple arithmetic progression, it would be virtually impossible to lose. If the progression were steeper than the example I've used, such as 1 2 4 7 11 16 22 (or) 2 4 6 8 10, it would be equally sure to win and profit would come faster. Nevertheless, I strongly advise against use of this system without major modification in actual play. The reward at the end of the rainbow could be much too small relative to the investment required.**

There are many other strategies in which the risk-reward factor is more promising. Some of these will be discussed in detail in subsequent chapters. I have no wish to labor this subject, but the widely accepted premise that a small minus expectancy cannot be overcome is utter nonsense. Without regard to systems or progressions, the player's advantages alone, if properly utilized, go a long way toward offsetting the house percentage. The player can select his bets, vary their amounts, and quit or pull back at a time of his own choosing.

Increasing Bets As One Loses (a sure way to lose?)

How often does one hear that this procedure amounts to sending good money after bad; that it has to be a losing proposition. I submit that the preceding section demonstrates quite clearly not only that it can win, but also that it is unquestionably one of the surest ways to win. Of course it has flaws, as do all systems.

*Last six decisions were passes.
**A mail-order promoter is currently selling this system as a "foolproof" way to win at Blackjack; price $20.

Any system that calls for recouping prior losses by increasing one's commitment is likely to fall into the "grind" category and to produce winnings more slowly than systems which pyramid their winning bets.

Nevertheless, if your primary object is to wind up on the plus side of the ledger rather than to see how much you can win in the shortest possible time, this is a perfectly sound way to go. You have only to formulate a series of 3 to a maximum of 9 or 10 progressively increasing bets in which a single win, a double win, or a parlay at any point will exceed or largely offset any preceding losses in the same series. Having done that, you must determine through testing whether you are justified in anticipating winnings sufficient to overcome the occasional losses of your whole series that are bound to occur from time to time.

Later on you will be shown several good systems employing this approach. Two or three of these, I am convinced, will overcome the player's minus expectancy in craps and single-zero roulette with some degree of consistency.

System Players: The House Loves 'Em?

How often one hears that comment. We're told that for 5,000 years mathematicians have tried in vain to invent a system which would win consistently in games of chance. Hogwash; we've just demonstrated that a simple arithmetic progression, impractical though it may be, solves this supposedly age-old problem. Moreover, the fact is that the great majority of people who gamble, including virtually all those who win, use some kind of system, conventional or otherwise. Casinos never claim that *all* of their customers are losers; even if that were true, it wouldn't be good for business.

The truth is that there are quite a few consistent winners — and every single member of that elite group must use a system, or perhaps two or three systems. They represent less than one percent of all casino patrons, and many of them are barred in places where they are known, but rest assured that without systems they might win occasionally, but never consistently —

and all casinos would welcome them with open arms.

A puzzling aspect of most treatises on the subject of systems is that the matter is generally approached in terms of geometric rather than arithmatic progressions. The authors concede that one would win ultimately if he just kept doubling his losing bets. And then they delight in showing that if he did that with a starting bet of $1, after 10 losses his 11th bet would have to be $1,024, which amount would return him the handsome profit of $1.

In his excellent book *The Weekend Gambler's Handbook*, Major Riddle of the Dunes Hotel in Vegas implies that all systems must lose. Then, paradoxically enough, he recommends two systems for craps, one or two for blackjack, and a basic system of money management.

Actually there are many systems that have real merit, and some of these — including partnerships in which the partners bet opposite to each other — will win on balance fairly consistently. The systems I refer to are based primarily on arithmatic rather than geometric progressions — but of course, none are represented as being perfect. They lose some of the time, but they'll show a net gain over a reasonable period. One characteristic they all share is "limited risk." No system can be good if it does not make allowance for occasional and inevitable losses.

"DICE HAVE NO MEMORIES"?

This theory — often expounded by the "experts" — tells us that since dice and the roulette wheel can't know what they've just finished doing, the next roll or spin has exactly the same chance of repeating, as if there had been no prior rolls or spins. Granted, that premise sounds logical, but let's take a closer look.

Suppose a coin tossed under laboratory conditions comes up heads six times in a row. You are then invited to write down three guesses as to the next three tosses, and promised a nice prize if any one of your guesses is correct. What would you have written on your piece of paper?* You may not have a scientific explanation for your guesses, but common sense probably told you that repeat sequences tend to get scarcer as they get longer.

If you believe, as I do, in the theory of "unequal distribution," you assume that the life expectancy of any thing or phenomenon must become progressively shorter as that thing or phenomenon grows older or lasts longer. Dice and the wheel are inanimate, but if their behavior were not subject to some governing force or principle, sequences of 30 or more repeats might be commonplace, and there could be no games like craps or roulette, because there would be no way of figuring probabilities and odds. I am convinced that there is a *law of diminishing probability* which is as valid as the law of averages. This theory or law, I believe, applies to any chance happening, and I am supported in my belief by the records of thousands of dice and roulette decisions.

My own records of 7,000-odd Las Vegas dice decisions (120–150 hours of continuous play) indicate that repeat or alternating sequences longer than 11 almost never happen, and that when such sequences have reached a length of 7, there tends to be a much sharper drop-off than the 50 percent prescribed by conventional wisdom and mathematical law.

An Englishman named Patrick O'Neil-Dunne has written a delightful book called *Roulette for the Millions*. In it he describes, analyzes, and documents, with typical British lucidity and thoroughness, a 31-day roulette marathon played in Macao off the coast of China near Hong Kong. In that marathon there were 20,800 spins of a single-zero wheel, and the longest recorded repeat run of any of the six even chances was 13. That length was reached on just three occasions. As a matter of fact, runs of 8 or more for each even chance averaged only 1 for every 650 spins. Since conventional math tells us that such runs should have occurred once every 256 spins, there is an

---

*If you wrote anything but "tails, tails, tails," arithmetic probably was not your best subject in school.

obvious and unexplained discrepancy. By itself, the single zero could not have created so large a discrepancy, and the book does not even tell us whether the zero was counted; nor does it tabulate and report the number of repeat runs of 5, 6, and 7. My own assumption is that it was that mystical figure 7; that as in dice, there was a surprisingly steep decline in the number of such sequences going beyond a length of 7.

Returning to my theory of "diminishing probability," let's assume that we've just had a series of seven consecutive passes at craps. At that point I would not argue that on the very next attempt the probability of a pass was materially less than 50 percent, but I would argue until blue in the face that in the next three attempts there would be far less than the normal 1 in 8 chance of three more passes. My records seem to show that the true odds in that situation would be more like 12½ to 1 against.

THE HOUSE PERCENTAGE IS MISLEADING

Since the purpose of this book is to help casino patrons to hold their own or better, I dislike having to sound a discouraging note. However, the best way to approach any project is to be armed with all the facts one can gather about that project. The sad truth is that the real house advantage in all casino games is always much greater than the so-called house percentage. On all even-money bets it is roughly twice the size of that percentage.

In craps the percentage is said to vary from a minimum of 0.6 percent on line bets with double odds to a high of about 16 percent. In roulette with two zeros the house edge is called 5.26 percent — and in blackjack it is impossible to pinpoint a specific figure because of the numerous variables. Depending upon the player's skill or lack thereof, the honesty of the management and/or the dealer, and the rules of the particular casino, the percentage can vary from zero to 20 percent or more.

Percentage figures are honest as far as they go, but they don't quite tell the story. We are told, for example, that the house edge against the line bettor in craps is 1.4 percent. However, in addition to that modest 1.4 advantage, the house obviously is entitled to win at least 50 percent of all even-chance bets. Let's see where that leaves our player. He's made 100 one-dollar bets and lost $1.40 to the house percentage. That left $98.60 to be divided between his right and wrong guesses. If his batting average was 50 percent, he will have won $49.30 while the casino will have won $50.70. The difference is still $1.40, but the percentage difference is not 1.4; it is more like 2.8 percent.

A roulette wheel provides a very clear example of this mathematical paradox. Suppose the wheel, instead of 37 or 38 numbers, had 40 numbers including zero and double zero. The house percentage then would be 2/40ths, or five percent. The house would be expected to win five of every 100 spins. That would leave 95 spins on which our player, betting red, had an exactly even chance. If he won 47½ of his bets, the house would have won 52½ bets. So again the difference expressed as a percentage is double the so-called house percentage.

WITH LIMITED RISK FUNDS, SHOULD YOU PLAY THE SLOTS, KENO, ETC.?

There is a tendency on the part of vacationers and others for whom gambling may be just a side issue, to gravitate toward the slot machines or the Keno section, or perhaps to mechanical horse races or blackjack. In all of these attractions the house "take" is much larger than in craps, roulette, or regular blackjack which offer superior opportuniy to win, plus more enjoyment while playing.

The average "take" of Las Vegas slot machines is said to be 20 percent — just like changing a $10 bill into 1 five and 3 ones. Lord only knows what the "take" is in Keno, but I'd have to guess that it is a good deal more than 20 percent. Granted, we hear quite frequently of fabulous jackpots, or of an enormous win at Keno, but let's face it, the odds are unattractive.

Many of the systems described in this book are suitable, or can easily be made suitable, for bankrolls as small as $30 to $50 when used in any one of the three major casino games.

In Nevada they have what they call 25¢ craps, meaning that the minimum chips in those games are 25¢ instead of the usual $1 — and that full odds are paid on small bets in multiples of 25¢. Minimum chips for roulette are often 10¢ and 25¢, while blackjack with minimums as low as 50¢ and $1 is available everywhere. The message is clear: unless your favorite hobby is philanthropy, avoid the odd-ball games, Keno, and the slots. By so doing, you will have given your chance of returning home a winner a 500 percent boost.

CHAPTER 2

Bet Selection

Don't be alarmed at the title of this chapter. I'm not going to offer some magic formula for guessing right more than 50 percent of the time — though I wish I could. Regrettably, there is no such formula. But there is a way to improve one's chances of being right at least 50 percent of the time, while at the same time reducing the frequency and the length of sequences of consecutive losing bets.

As I have already indicated, many sound systems call for increasing bets as one loses. In these systems, as well as some where bets are raised as one wins, switching from one side to the other — from pass to don't, or from red to black — can be essential if one hopes to avoid those ruinous adverse runs which are the bane of all gamblers, especially system players.

There are many theories on this subject, some of them plausible and some crackpot. There is the "dominance" theory, under which many gamblers bet that the dice or the little ivory ball will continue to do what it has been doing most recently. If two or three low numbers have just come up, you'll usually find most of the chips on the lower half of a roulette layout. If the dice miss three or four times, players will begin leaving the table, or they may start betting don't. If you accept the premise that luck tends to run in streaks, then this "dominance" theory makes some sense. That, I fear, cannot be said for those who stoutly maintain (1) that the next decision is most likely to be the same as the last decision; (2) that it will surely be the opposite of the last decision; or (3) that it will be whatever is favorable for the house and unfavorable for most of the players at the table — and so on.

I confess that when I walk up to a table I am influenced by

ailing atmosphere, the seeming confidence of the
and other externals, but I try always to temper my
to such things with the reflection that nothing in a
game of chance is quite as controlling as the good old law
of averages.

My basic method of bet selection is what I call the "Pattern."
It resembles the dominance theory but is much superior. With
it, your bets follow the current pattern of decisions. If they are
repeating you will be betting repeat; if they're alternating,
you'll be alternating right along with them. With this method,
you have to be on the right side of all very long sequences even
when they seem to defy the laws of probability. To accomplish
this *you need only make sure that each of your bets is the same as
the second preceding decision.*

The exact opposite of the Pattern is good when decisions
are choppy. Like the Pattern, it has the enormously important
virtue of tending to reduce the number of consecutive losses
caused by abnormally long repeat or alternating sequences.
Another attribute is that its winnings tend to come in pairs.
This can be important if one's money management system
calls for parlays or two successive wins at some point. I call
this method "Repeat-Reverse." If the last decision was a repeat, you bet alternate; if you win, your next bet would be
repeat, and so on. If you had lost that bet on alternate, you
would continue betting that the next decision would be opposite to the one just had until you won; then you'd bet repeat.

While winning with this "Reverse-Repeat" procedure, your
bets continue that way regardless of what the decision happens to be. Suppose you lose a bet on red to repeat; you must
now change and bet black, since it is the "repeat" that you
continue betting until you win; not the specific color or the
pass or don't pass.

Now I'll try to show you why and how these two methods
of bet selection work. Nearly all money-management systems
fail when they encounter a long string of consecutive adverse
decisions. Decisions themselves come in an infinite variety
of patterns, but the longest repetitive patterns are apt to be

repeats. For some reason, long sequences of alternating decisions tend to be somewhat shorter and less common than
lengthy repeat sequences, but they occur often enough. A
third and less common type of sequence is one of alternating
pairs, or doublets. These doublet sequences would hurt if
you were using the "Pattern" bet selection method, but they
would be perfect for "Repeat-Reverse."

In the examples that follow, + and − represent the outcome of any even-money proposition:

    1. Longest Runs + + + + + + + + or − − − − − − − −
    2. Next Longest − + − + − + − +
    3. Third Longest + + − − + + − − − − −

Line 1 has eight pluses; if the two preceding decisions had
been minuses and you were using the "Pattern," you'd have
lost your first two bets and won the next six. Had you been
betting "Repeat-Reverse," you would have won the first two
bets and lost the rest. If the immediately preceding decisions
had been + −, Pattern would have lost only its second bet in
that series of +s, while its opposite number would have won
only that same second bet. Note that these procedures have
shortened the number of possible successive losses by two.
If + represented the color black and you were betting red,
you would have lost eight bets in a row.

Line 2 shows eight alternating decisions. If you had been
betting repeat all the way, you'd have lost eight successive
bets. Using Pattern, you would have lost the second bet and
won the rest, while with its opposite number, you'd have
won the second bet and lost the rest.

As for Line 3, Pattern had to lose at least seven of the first
eight bets, while Repeat-Reverse was winning at least seven
of eight. Of course, Pattern would have won the last four bets
in that line. Again the number of possible consecutive losses
or wins for both methods was limited to the length of the sequence minus 2.

Both these methods are safer and decidedly preferable to
random selection or sticking to one side or the other continu-

ously. You will recall that series of Las Vegas dice decisions in which there were only four passes in 27 attempts. While that was happening, if you had been using Repeat-Reverse, you had to win at least eight of your bets instead of only four if you'd been betting the pass line. That ratio of losses to wins would have been 19 to 8 instead of 23 to 4.

Both methods will produce a roughly .500 batting average, but due to periodic long runs of repeat or alternating sequences, Repeat-Reverse is the riskier of the two. When using it, one should always be alert for anything that "smells" like an incipient run and be prepared either to "change horses in midstream" or to skip a bet or two. Long runs seem to breed more long runs, and when a table is choppy, it frequently tends to stay that way for quite a while. In craps, if a new shooter rolls one or two 7s on his initial come-out, or if there are three or more consecutive passes or don'ts, these can be signals for caution it often pays to heed.

Perhaps the simplest way of conveying my thought here is this: if you're doing nicely with one of these selection procedures, stay with it. If you're doing poorly, you know, of course, that would not be the case if you were using its opposite number — so consider the advisability of switching systems. Flexibility often is a decisive factor in the success or failure of any venture, and it can be a great asset whenever the going gets a bit rough in one of these casino games.

At this point I suspect you're saying to yourself, "I'd like to try these selection or switching methods, but how the devil am I to keep track of what my next bet should be?" Well, you can relax, for that is surprisingly easy to do.

You buy chips of two different denominations. They will be easy to distinguish because their colors will be different. Your plan will be to rack those chips or stack them in an arrangement by color that corresponds exactly to the pattern of recent decisions. The red chips may represent passes and the white chips misses. At the crap table you have two racks for your chips, and one of those can be used for this purpose. Then all you have to remember is that the *second preceding decision is the one to watch*. You bet that same way if you're using "Pattern," and the opposite way for "Repeat-Reverse."

For roulette, you will probably want to watch all six of the even propositions, and maybe the "dozens" and "columns" as well. In that case your chips won't help, but a simple running record in a small notebook can be very helpful. In the chapter on that game we'll deal with that. If your interest is confined to the colors, or high/low or odd/even, then you can stack your multi-colored chips to reflect each spin.

I do not wish to overemphasize the importance of these two methods of bet selection, but I can tell you that my own typical casino experience improved markedly after I discovered them. For any system whose success hinges upon choice of the right even-money bet, they cannot, in my opinion, be improved upon. Even if one shifts from one to the other of these methods, as I do quite often, he will find that some degree of adherence to whichever formula he likes at the moment will usually yield better results than pure guesses.

Here are two hypothetical series of dice decisions; + representing pass and — representing don't pass. See if you can tell which method would be best for each series, and correctly write down your wins (W) and losses (L) using that method beginning with the third decision in each series. (Answers at bottom of page.)

    Series "A" — — + — — + + — — — + + + — — + — + — — — + +
                — — +
    Series "B" — + — + — — — + + + + — — + — + — + — — — — —
                + — +

I'm sure you scored perfectly on this little test, but if you did not, the correct answers will show you where and why you slipped up.

Series "A" (Reverse-Repeat): WLWWWWWLWWLWWWLLLWLWW
WWW
Series "B" (Pattern): WWWLWLLWWLLLWWWWWLWWWLWW

CHAPTER 3

Odds and Probabilities

A basic understanding of percentages and the laws of probability can be quite helpful to anyone who gambles. They tell him when to hold back or when to plunge, and which games and which bets in those games are the most promising. They can also enable him to improvise mathematically sound money-management systems for himself.

If a player knows that on even propositions the odds against making five correct guesses in a row are 31 to 1, he also knows that the same 31 to 1 odds must apply to his chance of guessing wrong five times in succession. If he realizes that there is little likelihood of his winning 50 percent of his bets in blackjack, he must also realize that to have a fair chance of coming out ahead in that game, he should split pairs and double down whenever favorable situations arise. He knows that in craps, if repeat sequences of five passes or misses occur an average of once every 30-odd decisions, that the chance of a long roll — 15 or more numbers — between 7s must be equally good since 7s have only a 1 in 6 probability of appearing on any roll, while as between passes or misses, each has a 1 in 2 chance of being the next decision.

If some well-meaning friend comes along with a great new idea for "cleaning up" at one of the casino games, our man who knows his odds and percentages isn't likely to be ensnared if the idea is unsound.

I am reminded of a personal experience years ago when I was young and innocent — and before I'd ever seen the inside of a casino. A friend with whom I was weekending knew a sure-fire way to win at craps. All you had to do, he said, was to bet pass, and when you won, let your winnings ride three

TABLE 1
Probability of Even Chances Repeating or Alternating

Exact number of times (no more)	Specific chance to repeat or alternate	Number of times (or more)	Either chance to repeat or alternate	Specific chance to repeat or alternate
2	1:7	2	1:1	1:3
3	1:15	3	1:3	1:7
4	1:31	4	1:7	1:15
5	1:63	5	1:15	1:31
6	1:127	6	1:31	1:63
7	1:255	7	1:63	1:127
		8	1:127	1:255
		9	1:255	1:511

times (a three-stage parlay). In other words, play for four consecutive passes. This would return a $150 profit on your initial $10 wager — and you couldn't miss in 10 tries, he assured me. The prospect was intriguing, but things didn't work out quite as planned even though we gave the idea a thorough test — perhaps as many as 40 or 50 tries. Because I had not stopped to consider the odds against calling any even chance four times consecutively, I learned a fairly costly lesson. Those odds happen to be 15 to 1.

Success in any venture requires constant and careful evaluation of risks and rewards, and this is especially true in games of chance. To gamble without some understanding of percentages and odds may not always be suicidal, but it always compounds the odds against the gambler, and it is usually foolish.

The odds pertaining to even chances have a direct bearing on at least 90 percent of all casino wagers. If you know those odds, you can generally compute or estimate odds when the chances are better or less than even. In Table 1 you are shown the odds against repeat and alternating sequences of any even-money proposition.

TABLE 2
Odds on Specific Bets Involving Even Chances

Number of trials	To call all or none	Correctly call 1 or more	Correctly call 2 or more
2	1:3	3:1	1:3
3	1:7	7:1	1:1
4	1:15	15:1	11:5
5	1:31	31:1	26:6*
6	1:63	63:1	
7	1:127	127:1	
9	1:511	511:1	

*In extensive tests with preferred bet selection procedures, these odds increased to 5¼:1.

Table 2 shows the odds on specific bets involving even chances.

Table 3 shows actual statistics on repeat runs of passes and misses based on approximately 5,000 decisions, of which 3,900 took place on the Las Vegas Strip and 1,100 were borrowed from H.B. Adams' "3400 Casts of the Dice" in his book *The Guide to Gambling*.

The Table 3 figures show that:

Runs of 5 or more occurred once in 36 decisions

Runs of 7 or more occurred once in 140 decisions

Runs of 8 or more occurred once in 450+ decisions

Alternating sequences of comparable length occurred less frequently than repeat sequences, but there were almost equal numbers of such sequences 8 and over in length.

My own experience and testing have indicated that in craps whenever we've had five to seven repeats, or four alternating decisions, the odds will be quite favorable if we bet that those sequences will not continue for three additional decisions. A three-stage Martingale such as 5-10-20 would be appropriate in these situations. (Note: Table 3 figures show that of 139

TABLE 3
Number of Repeat Sequences in 5,000 Dice Decisions (Pass and Don't Pass)

Length of sequence	5	6	7	8	9	10	11	more
Number of occurrences	76	27	25	6	1	2	2	0

repeat runs 5 or longer, only 11 reached a length of eight repeats or more. *12½ to 1 odds on a normally 7 to 1 bet are inviting*.)

As for roulette repeat sequences, my records of Nevada spins are too limited to be considered conclusive. However, 1,426 spins give us 4,278 decisions for the three sets of even chances, red/black, high/low and odd/even. Repeat sequences in those 4,000 odd decisions are shown in Table 4.

Thus the average ratio for each of the three sets of even chances was not too dissimilar from the above dice ratios. Also, as with dice, alternating runs of similar length were noticeably less frequent than repeat runs.

> Repeat runs of 5 or longer occurred once in 42 decisions
> Repeat runs of 6 or longer occurred once in 78 decisions
> Repeat runs of 7 or longer occurred once in 142 decisions
> Repeat runs of 8 or longer occurred once in 237 decisions
> Repeat runs of 9 or longer occurred once in 534 decisions

The two zeros on Nevada wheels of course had some effect on the above numbers, but re-examination of data in O'Neil-Dunne's *Roulette For The Millions* suggests that the extra zero did not have a major impact on repeat sequences. In his 20,800 spins of a single-zero wheel, the longest recorded such run was 13 — and runs of 8 or more on each of the three sets of even chances averaged only 1 in 325 spins — considerably less frequent than my Nevada ratio.

These figures do not reveal any potentially bargain-basement bets as attractive as the craps bet suggested above. However, a three-stage Martingale bet that any repeat or alternating run 3 to 5 in length will not continue three more times would make sense.

TABLE 4
Number of Repeat Sequences of Even Chances in 4,278 Roulette Decisions

Length of sequence	5	6	7	8	9	10	11	more
Number of occurrences	46	26	12	10	4	2	2	0

One of the most peculiar but intriguing betting ploys I have ever seen was at the Victoria Sporting Club in London a few years ago. A man sat down at my table and placed one chip each on all six of the even chances. He couldn't win and he couldn't lose unless the single 0 came up, in which case he would lose half his bets. Otherwise, he had to win three bets and lose three. But after each spin he replaced his losing chips and left his winnings on the table (parlayed his winning bets). Within less than an hour he cashed in a hatfull of chips — enough to indicate that he had hit either three runs of six repeats, two runs of seven repeats, or one run of eight repeats. Those sequences would have yielded profits of 189, 254, or 255 British pounds, respectively.

The foregoing data and the tabulations on repeat sequences may prove of some value to the "spot" or "situation" bettor, and also to the player who never seems to realize that there are times when discretion is the better part of valor, when money still at risk should be gathered up and bets sharply reduced. He must learn to think of gambling as a contest between himself and the casino. As in war, football, or tennis, he must occasionally lose a battle, a touchdown, or a game — but if he protects his reserves by limiting his risk in any single gambit, lady luck and/or the good old law of averages or both are likely to re-assert themselves at some point and help him to emerge victorious.

Now let's briefly consider systems or progressions in which two wins or two successive wins are needed for a successful coup. In some ways this approach is more practical than the one-win approach. The profit potential of two wins in a series of 5 or 6 bets can bear a relatively respectable ratio to total risk.

And that ratio can be dramatically improved if the two wins are consecutive. Trying for two wins instead of one obviously reduces the probability of success — but to what extent?

In my search for a formula by which to compute the probability of a double win in any given number of trials, I have drawn a complete blank. I have read 15 library books on the mathematics of probability, including one that is regarded as the "Bible" in that field — and I've consulted a half dozen Ph.D.'s at UCLA, USC, Systems Development Corp., and Computer Sciences Corporation, all without usable result. Of the half-dozen different answers given by the experts, several were so wide of the mark they were laughable. I am therefore left with no choice but to fall back on my own considerable testing and experimenting — and my own logic.

The chance of calling any even proposition correctly twice in succession is exactly 25 percent — the product of one's chance on his first try multiplied by his chance on the second try, 50 percent times 50 percent. That probably explains one "expert" opinion that in six consecutive attempts at such a parlay, "one's probability of success would be 1½ to 1."

Though I've long since forgotten most of my school algebra and calculus, I hope that I am still able to think logically. In all events, here is the way I approach the problem of the correct odds for or against one successful parlay in six tries:

You have a 50 percent chance of being right on any even bet. If you make six such bets in a row, your average number of wins should be three. If you have three wins, there must be an exactly even chance that each of those wins will be followed by a second win. The odds in favor of making one correct call in three tries are 7 to 1. This ratio corresponds pretty closely to the 6 to 1 success ratio I have had with the Parlay Progression you will meet later on.

Table 5 reflects the mathematical basis for several betting systems I have used with varying degrees of success. Full descriptions of these systems will be found in the chapter entitled "Winning Progressions." Meanwhile, this data should be of interest. The figures are close approximations,

TABLE 5
Adjusted Odds on Various Propositions*

5-number bet series	Win no bets: 2 to 3%; odds against: 40:1 Win 1 bet only: 16%; odds against: 5¼:1 Win 2 bets or more: 84%; odds for: 5¼:1
9-number double win series	Approximately 60 wins for each loss of series, treating each double win as 1 win and each single win of the first number in the series as 1 win; odds: 60:1
7-number parlay series	Chances for 1 successful parlay in 6 attempts; odds for: 429:72 or 6:1
10-number parlay series	Chances for 1 successful parlay in 9 attempts; odds for: 474:27 or 17½:1

*Using preferred bet selection procedures in Chapter 2.

and it should be noted that these figures, unlike those in Table 1, are based almost entirely on extensive but unscientific tests made by myself.

In the Table 5 double-win and parlay series, the first bet was repeated until it lost, at which point the double-win and parlay attempts began. The odds or ratios shown for the two parlay series do not include those first-bet wins, which turned out to be almost equal in number to the total number of successful parlays. According to the widely held thesis that what they've done in the past has absolutely no bearing on what the dice or the wheel will do next, the fact that in these series a losing bet always preceded the double-win and parlay attempts was irrelevant and had no effect on the test results. As previously indicated, in achieving those results I used my own pet methods of bet selection. In many instances the two opposing methods were applied to the same set of dice decisions, the intention being to try for results as truly indicative as possible of what might be expected in casino play. It should be recognized, however, that my own results may differ materially from expectations based on pure mathematics, random methods of bet selection, or betting the same way continuously.

In view of the enormous amount of written material on the

subjects of probability and permutations and combinations, it is strange that so little of it has any practical value for patrons of games of chance. This is especially puzzling since these games are so frequently used by writers to illustrate their theories. For example, how much deviation from the norm should one expect in 50, 100, or 500 trials of an even chance? I know of no formula that will provide an answer, but my own experience suggests *outer limits* of about 40 percent in 50 trials, 20 percent in 100 trials, and perhaps five percent to seven percent in 500 trials. I also have an impression that the degree and frequency of extreme deviation is likely to be greater in roulette and blackjack than in craps.

If my guesses on deviation limits are not too far off the mark, it follows that deviation norms are in the area of one-fourth or one-fifth the above extremes. This means that in 100 trials — less than 2 hours play in most casino games — average deviation might be in the 5 percent range. There are some systems whose success require a high degree of short-range divergence from the norm, while other systems win when results "go according to the book." Any really good system in the last category should perform nicely when deviation is no more than 5 or 6 percent.

I believe it is absolutely essential to heed and respect the laws of probability. The old bromide to the effect that "casinos make their money from brave losers and cowardly winners" is just that — a bromide — possibly originated and given currency by the casinos themselves.

Not long ago I watched a young man begin play at a crap table with $500 of green ($25) chips. He was using the conventional pass—come—take the odds system, and luck was with him. Soon there were 10 or 15 black ($100) chips in his rack and his bets were $100 plus double odds. Then came one of the fabulous runs that crapshooters dream about. The shooter made only about five passes, but in the process, and without rolling a single 7, he hit not less than 40 place numbers. (On average, a 7 should appear once in six rolls.) Our hero took full advantage; he not only kept increasing his line and come bets, he also "placed" all of the numbers, so that throughout most of that run he had 14 separate bets on the table. Whenever a number was hit he would "press" (double his bet on that number), usually taking back a few $5 or $25 chips in change. However, when the shooter finally 7nd out, our man had not drawn down a single winning bet — and he had left on the table not less than $20,000. This, of course, was an extreme example of greed or excessive optimism, but I'm sure that episodes like it happen many times each day at crap tables in Las Vegas.

I think of luck itself as being a chance happening subject to the same permutations as other chance occurrences. Its distributional patterns will vary not only from day to day and month to month, but also from half-hour to half-hour. To play as if each time luck smiles at you the millenium had finally arrived, is to court repeated disappointment. Take advantage of it, by all means — but do so in short spurts, for it can be mighty fickle.

One of the best ways I know for improving one's overall results is to resolve that his quitting time will, whenever possible, be at a moment when things are going favorably for him. If you know you will have to stop playing in 15 or 20 minutes and you're enjoying a bit of good luck at this moment, the time to quit is right now. Never forget that a player has just three basic options with which to combat the casino's obvious advantages: (1) he can choose his bets; (2) he can determine the size of his bets; and (3) he can elect to quit whenever he pleases. By quitting when his fortunes are on an upswing, he may miss the crest of the wave, but more importantly, he is sure to miss the trough.

CHAPTER 4

Psychology and Tactics

Systems and betting psychology are directly related. Although the variations in different systems are just about endless, all of them except those of the multiple-bet variety in craps and roulette fall into one or two basic categories. The first category relies primarily on the normal functioning of the law of averages; the second on occasional sharp deviation from the norm. The cautious player tends to pin his hopes on mathematical probabilities, while his opposite number attempts to cash in on those mathematical abnormalities sure to make their appearance from time to time.

There are just two generic types of betting systems: (1) up-as-you-win; and (2) up-as-you-lose. Both approaches have undeniable merit, though conventional wisdom holds that it is foolish to increase bets when losing. We'll take another look at both sides of this question:

If you escalate your bets when winning, your first risk can be your only risk. Luck comes and goes in streaks, and when it smiles, the way to take full advantage is to jump your bets and your betting level as rapidly as you can, using money that wasn't yours to begin with. In any two-hour period there should be several favorable runs which, with this procedure, can yield profits that more than offset prior losses. This is the typical optimist's viewpoint and — let's face it — if you're willing to risk serious money in these games, you are optimistic. With this approach one can win many times the amount of his stake in very little time — but to do so he needs more than an average amount of luck.

If the anticipated series of favorable sequences doesn't arrive before one's bankroll has evaporated or been severely dented; if results are choppy (alternating wins and losses without long runs); or if one has pressed his luck too hard and failed to cash in winnings before they became losses — then the policy of stepping up one's bets while winning can become extremely frustrating. To summarize, the up-as-you-win method accounts for nearly all the really big killings made in casino gambling, but it is also a major, if not *the* major, contributor to casino profits. An over-optimistic player can easily win 55 to 60 percent of his wagers and still wind up a loser. Why else do you suppose that virtually all casinos extend V.I.P. treatment including air fare, rooms, shows, escorts and food, etc. to high rollers and gambling junketeers?

Now let's examine the other basic approach. A player who has a healthy respect for the law of averages realizes that he is quite likely to win less than 50 percent of his bets, and he wants a system with which he has a good chance to win if his luck is only so-so and his guesses are less than 50 percent correct. He recognizes the immediate improbability of the probable, but he also knows the long odds against making four, five, or more consecutive wrong guesses on any even proposition. He will attempt to recover losses when they occur by increasing his subsequent bets. Of course, if he is prudent he will limit his risk in any single series of losses to a fraction of his stake so that an occasional loss of a series or "bank" will not affect his ability to continue play.

The drawbacks to this type of play are several. Winnings come relatively slowly, and since the laws of probability can be fickle, they cannot be counted upon to be functioning each time their assistance is urgently needed. Most up-as-you-lose systems fall into what may be called the "grind" category. Moreover, one or two series of successive losses can wipe out profits that took hours to accumulate. Despite these negative factors, however, I am convinced that intelligent application of this basic approach will produce good results on balance and at least as good a ratio of wins to losses as the opposite approach.

In my judgment flexibility, the willingness and ability to "swim with the tide" is the real key and the most important ingredient of success at the tables. Naturally, I like to win rapidly, and whenever possible, to be betting with the house's money, so my usual procedure when I first arrive at a table is to escalate my bets when winning. However, I am essentially cautious. I generally draw down enough of each winning bet, except possibly the first two bets of a series, so that when the inevitable loss occurs, my net gain will have equalled or exceeded the profit I'd have had if all my bets had been "flat" (all the same amount). I suppose my desire to win something is stronger than my ambition to win a great deal, for quite often when an exceptionally good run is in progress, I will pull back or pull out well before it has ended.

If my initial efforts fail to prove profitable in 15 or 20 minutes, I'm quite likely to shift gears and begin trying to overcome losses by increasing my bets. A willingness to be flexible, to attempt to "swim with the tide," will often pay handsome dividends.

Sometimes in the course of four or five hours of play, I will have switched from one of several betting systems to another a half-dozen times. There is no single system that is always right for all occasions and all the exigencies that can arise in the course of a prolonged session at the tables.

Your own choice of systems should harmonize as closely as possible with conditions of the moment in the game you're playing, and should also suit your own basic psychology and circumstances. Within these pages you will find an exceptionally broad spectrum of systems selected with care and with the specific design of satisfying the needs of any casino patron, no matter what those needs may be.

CHAPTER 5

Conventional Systems and Some Recommended Variations

The systems discussed in this chapter are suitable for the even-money bets in craps and roulette. While some of them can be adapted to blackjack, they are not, per se, recommended for that game.

Roulette as played on the French and Italian Rivieras in the eighteenth and nineteenth centuries is responsible for most of the glamorously named systems which we now regard as "old hat" or conventional. You are not likely to encounter any money-management system, ingenious or otherwise, which isn't based on the same principles as those old systems handed down to us by our not-so-dumb forefathers. Among the best known and most widely used of these, are the following:

D'ALENBERT

In which bets are raised one unit after each losing bet and lowered one unit after each winning bet, thus assuring that winning bets will always be larger than losing bets. This system promises a profit of about one-half unit for each bet made, provided that wins and losses are fairly evenly divided.

D'Alenbert, however, is less innocuous than it may appear. Suppose your stake is $100 or $150 and you start with a $1 bet. It would not be at all unusual for you to win only 10 of your first 30 bets, at which point you would have lost about $50 and be called upon to risk 10 to 20 percent of your remaining funds on each additional bet you made. I've experimented with this system in its original form several times and have never been too impressed.

At 60 decisions per hour, spacing bets $1 apart, you win nearly $30 per hour if all goes well. Then along comes an adverse run which may last only ten or fifteen minutes, and two hours of profits will have evaporated.

Like so many systems designed to recapture losses by raising the amount one bets, this one tends to lull you into a sense of false security with its steady flow of small profits. Nevertheless, the principle is sound and I shall now show you a couple of D'Alenbert variations which seem to hold up pretty well:

1. Using constant spacing between the numbers, limit your bet series to no more than 9 or 11 digits. Begin by betting the middle number in the series. Whenever you lose either the high or the low bet in your series, start again at the middle number.

2. Use a sequence such as 1 2 3 4 7 11 17 in which a win of any two consecutive numbers will offset any possible prior losses. Start with the lowest number using regular D'Alenbert, but when you win two successive bets or lose the top number in the series, go back to that low number. This procedure seems to be better than number 1 above, and you can win fairly consistently even if your luck is only so-so. Furthermore, unless the pattern of decisions is very abnormal, two partners playing this system and betting opposites can both win. In the following hypothetical series of decisions, there are 6 +s and 10 −s, yet if one partner bet the +s and the other the −s, each of them would wind up with a net profit of 7 units:

$$- \ - + - + - - + - - - + - - + +$$

MARTINGALE

This is the system in which bets are doubled after each loss (1 2 4, etc.), thus assuring an ultimate profit equal to the first digit in the Martingale series, provided the player keeps on betting until he wins. Obviously this one can be dynamite. If you're playing to win $5, your bet sequence would be 5 10

20 40 80 so, having theoretically lost five successive bets, your next bet is $160. Playing to win $1, a run of seven losses would call for a $128 wager to recoup — and your loss at that point would be 127 times the amount you hoped to win.

However, Martingale limited to a series of three bets, or at most, four, sometimes makes a lot of sense. As stated previously, it is ideal for "spot" bets per my theory of diminishing probability, when any sequence has become abnormally long. As a matter of fact, a three-stage Martingale against continuation of any alternating sequence of the even chances in craps or roulette would always be a reasonable bet — and if such a sequence had already extended through three, four, or more decisions, the true odds, I maintain, would be considerably better than the "book" odds of 7 to 1.

When I first decided to try the "Pattern" method of switching bets from pass to don't pass, I spent two days in Vegas confining my gambling almost entirely to a variation of Martingale. I used a 10-10-20 bet series in which I bet 20 only after two consecutive losses of 10. Doing that I won about $500 in roughly eight hours of play, nine at most. That $62 per hour average may have been attributable to more than my fair share of luck. But this simple little system does seem to have merit, for I've used it several times since with satisfactory results. I've also used bet series of 5-10-20 and 5-10-15 in the same way, but never experienced results quite as good as with 10-10-20.

GRAND MARTINGALE

This is the same as Martingale except that to each doubled bet there is added one or more units, so that the bettor's prospective profit increases as he moves up his series. My comments on pure Martingale are generally applicable. The premise that reward ought to increase right along with risk is certainly valid, but in all up-as-you-lose systems, it seems that those two variables keep a more or less constant relationship. If one is increased, the other will increase automatically and proportionately — that is, unless one is willing to bide his time and skip some bets while waiting for a favorable situation.

The odds are 31 to 1 that you can't call any even proposition either correctly or incorrectly five times in a row. Let's say that you have just skipped a bet, intending to wait for a decision which you would have lost, had you continued. When that decision comes along, you propose to resume using a four-stage Martingale or Grand Martingale on the premise that the odds are still 31 to 1 in your favor even though the risk you intend to assume is only 1 in 16. Mathematicians will argue that you gained nothing by waiting, that the odds remained constant no matter what had transpired previously; but I've seen convincing evidence to the contrary.

I have been a net winner using these two Grand Martin-gale series on pass and don't pass in craps, 5-15-35-75 and 3-8-20-45. Generally my procedure has been to wait for what would have been a losing bet before beginning my series. When I win at any point in the series, I go back to the low bet and keep right on with that number until I lose. At that point I stop and wait for one or two successive results which would have been losses if I'd been betting. I then resume — again, with the low bet in my series. As a matter of fact, I can't recall losing when I've used this procedure, but it can be boring.*

LABOUCHERE OR SPLIT MARTINGALE

This is also known as the "Cancellation" system or the "1 2 3" system, in which the bettor picks a series of two, three, four, or more numbers which add up to the unit profit he expects to make. He then bets the total of the two outside numbers of his series and if he wins, he cancels those two numbers. He continues betting the two outside uncancelled numbers until each number in the series has been cancelled,

---

*I subsequently developed a more practical (and less boring) procedure embodying this same principle. You will find it on page 79 labeled "Super Martingale."

at which point he will have accomplished his mission. Whenever he loses a bet, the amount of his loss is added to his bet series as a single number. Thus he must cancel out two numbers for each number added — and he knows that unless his losses exceed his wins by a margin of almost 2 to 1, sooner or later all those numbers will be cancelled.

This is by long odds the most fascinating and the most *insidious* of all the old-time systems. It is said to have been responsible for more suicides on the French Riviera than all other systems combined. Not only does it produce a steady flow of small winnings for its users, but the logic behind it is so utterly transparent and the end results seemingly inevitable, that it becomes extremely difficult to resist the temptation to keep on with it even after an adverse run has pushed one's bets to a level beyond his means.

Labouchere has the appearance and the feel of being a 2 to 1 proposition on an even-money bet. But it really isn't; you don't get paid twice as much as you can lose. There is a world of difference between that and merely cancelling two numbers which represent exactly the amount you had at risk. In a long Labouchere series, the bets keep getting bigger even when wins and losses are evenly divided, so as the series progresses, the risk of reaching the table limit or your own limit increases steadily.

Suppose your Labouchere series was 1 2 3 4 (to yield a $10 unit profit) and you encountered the same sequence of wins and losses that produced a $7 gain for the second D'Alenbert bet series shown above. After your final two wins, you would have been minus $18, with your next bet scheduled to be $28. That would give you your $10 profit, if won. However, let's now assume that of your next six bets, your only win was bet number three. At that point you would be out $214 and your next bet would be $92. This will give you some idea of the speed with which losses can mount and bets escalate.

REVERSE LABOUCHERE

In London a few years ago, I recall having picked up a book in which Labouchere was analyzed in depth. The author concluded that a player using it might expect to lose (that is to be required to bet a sum beyond the usual house limit of £200 — $500) about once every 1,500 to 1,600 spins of a roulette wheel. On the Continent and in England, where the spin rate is roughly 30 per hour, that estimate implied one loss of anything from $1,000 to $3,000 or more, every 50 hours or so. In this country, with our two zeros and much faster spin rate, I'd have to guess that the loss ratio would be less inviting than 1 in 1,500 spins.

In 1976 William Morrow & Co. published a fascinating narrative, said to be true, entitled *Thirteen Against The Bank*. The author, a Britisher named Norman Leigh, recounts the story of his extraordinary and successful effort to beat the casinos by playing Labouchere in reverse. This meant adding the amount of each win to his bet series, and cancelling the two outside numbers each time he lost. Each bet was the total of those two outside numbers. This procedure, of course, entailed acceptance of a large number of very small losses in return for an occasional win averaging more than 1,000 times the amount at risk. A prime factor in his success was the smallness of his initial stakes. His 1 2 3 4 series represented either shillings or French francs equal to $1.40 or $2, respectively. In Nevada and elsewhere in this hemisphere, the same series used on the even chances in roulette would normally call for a $10 initial risk on each attempt. Either that or the maximum bet allowed would be much lower than the maximum Leigh was permitted to bet. So the vastly less favorable risk-reward ratio here would almost certainly defeat any attempt to duplicate his feat on this side of the Atlantic.

Nevertheless, the underlying principle of reverse Labouchere, controlled escalation of winning bets, coupled with strict limitation of loss, is widely accepted and used here. Every up-as-you-win progression embodies that same general principle, but the problems of control without pencil and paper, of extremely slow escalation at the beginning, accelerating only as one's series "mushrooms," and of finding a way to limit loss on a single series to as little as 1/1000th of average potential profit are not easily solved. Solving this problem poses a real challenge, and I confess that if one day I am ever fortunate enough to find the answer, I'll try to resist any temptation to broadcast it. After all, who in his right mind would intentionally destroy the source of all those prospective "golden eggs"?

In case my explanation of regular Labouchere needs clarification, here are two examples of the procedure:

Assume that we are playing to win units of $6. Our starting bet series could be 1 2 3 or 2 2 2 or 3 3. We'll make it 1 2 3. All bets are the total of the two outside uncancelled numbers, so our first bet is 4. We lose and add the 4 to our series, which now becomes 1 2 3 4. Next bet is 5 and we lose. Then we lose our third bet of 6 and our series is now 1 2 3 4 5 6. Then we win a bet and the series looks like this: 1̶ 2 3 4 5 6̶. After those three losses, we had to bet 7 and you can see that having won that bet, if we win our next two bets we will have cancelled all the numbers in our series. We will then have lost three bets and won three and reached our objective of a $6 profit. Now suppose we've had an adverse run and made 25 bets without completing our series. This is the way it might look:

1̶ 2̶ 3̶ 4̶ 5̶ 6̶ 8̶ 11̶ 14̶ 16̶ 21̶ 26̶ 29̶ 37̶ 45 61̶ 77̶ 74 103 132

We've lost 17 bets and won 8 and as you can see, our next bet is 177 — 45 plus 132. Not only does the addition get tougher, but it becomes increasingly difficult to quickly find the right uncancelled numbers as the series grows longer, while the time between spins (or bets) seems to grow shorter.

THE PARLAY

The name of this system is probably from the French or Italian word *Paroli*. It applies to the method of pyramiding profits by leaving winnings on the table throughout a series of two, three, or more bets. In this way $10 wagered becomes $40 after two successive wins; *i.e.*, a single successful parlay on an even-money bet consists of two successive and successful bets and yields a profit of three times the amount at risk. Parlays are used and decidedly useful in a wide variety of systems.

As an example of how parlays work, I was at a crap table on the Las Vegas Strip one day when I noticed a pile of about 30 $5 chips on the table right in front of me. I asked the man next to me if they were his and when he said they were mine, I couldn't have been more surprised. I had inadvertently left a single chip on the pass line and five successive passes had parlayed that chip into 32 chips. I grabbed them just in time, for the shooter missed on his next try. This incident illustrates how the parlay was originally used in roulette.

A roulette player who wishes to relax comfortably without stress or strain will find the parlay an ideal vehicle. He can bet on his favorite color risking an average of one chip every two spins of the wheel while waiting for a long run of that color. Or he can risk one chip per spin and always be in a position to take advantage of a long run of either color, or any other pair of even chances.

I am told that a recently published book recounts the story of a man who is supposed to have earned a good living for 30 years doing nothing but grinding out small hourly winnings with the following parlay series:

1 1 1 2 2 4 4 8 8 (total risk $31)

He would bet the first 1 until he lost; then he would move up the series, trying for a successful parly on each of the remaining numbers. The process would be repeated whenever he made his parlay or lost the whole series. You may have observed that a win on four of those eight parlay numbers would have yielded a net profit of only 1. Since about 50 percent of all his wins were sure to come on the first 1, chances are that when he didn't lose the whole series, his average profit was in the neighborhood of 2. However tedious and slow this means of self support may have been, you will see later that the underlying principle has real merit.

ASCOT

Winning bets are escalated one number at a time and losing bets lowered one number in an arbitrarily arranged series of seven to eleven numbers such as 2 3 5 ⑧ 13 20 30. In this series the first bet would be 8, the middle number, and whenever the last number, 30 in this case, was won or lost, the player would start over.

The problem with Ascot is that alternating wins and losses at the upper end of any series can destroy the profit potential. This can be a serious flaw in any progressive system calling for substantial pull-back after losses.

STRAIGHT-UP

Another method of escalating bets when winning is to move up a predetermined series of five to seven bets until the first loss, at which point the player starts over. This doubtless is as old a system as the others I've been describing, but so far as I know, it has no name, glamorous or otherwise. "Straight-Up" describes it, so we'll call it just that.

The conservative way of using this procedure is to require two consecutive wins of equal amounts before moving up a bet series. This serves to neutralize the net effect of alternate wins and losses. Beyond the first two bets, if one's upward progression is not too steep, his profit at any point where he loses before completing the series, will equal or nearly equal the profit he'd have had if all bets had been the same amount as his first two bets. For example, take the series 5 5 7 10 15 22 30. If he wins the whole series he'll be plus 94, but if he loses any bet from the third to the seventh in his series, he will still have a net profit roughly equal to or greater than if all his bets had been 5.

This system is basically more conservative than most of

those previously described, but for it to win, the element of luck is much more essential than it is for the others. It will win faster (but much less frequently) than the others — but losses, when they occur, are likely to be relatively light.

Every serious gambler who likes to jump his bets when he wins — and that includes most of us — has been perplexed at one time or another by the question of whether to escalate rapidly or slowly. If done slowly, occasional losses can be taken in stride. They need not wipe out previously accumulated profits — and if one has a few good sequences of winning bets bunched together, he can wind up with a nice profit.

On the surface, rapid escalation of winning bets seems needlessly risky. You win 5 and 15; and if your next bet, 25, is lost, you show a net deficit even though you've won two bets while losing only one. I have often wrestled with this problem and finally concluded that moderately fast escalation improves one's chances of emerging a winner. He doesn't have to win 60 or 70 percent of all his wagers; he can win 51 percent or even 48 percent as long as he is able — and willing — to terminate most of his scaled-up betting sequences with two, three, four, or more successive wins.

He should not, however, press his luck too hard. When those successive wins come along, if he's prudent he will chalk up his profit and sharply reduce the amount of his bets. By doing this he is making sure that his average winning bet is materially larger than his average losing bet. You will win three or more bets in a row quite often, but seldom if ever will you win 60 percent of all your bets in a session. Of course, there are times when you get 20 or more successive hits on the numbers at craps, but those occasions come all too infrequently to be relied upon.

CHAPTER 6

Winning Progressions

O ne day in Las Vegas I ran into a woman I knew only slightly, but whom I knew to be an inveterate gambler. She always implied that she won more or less consistently, but on this occasion she was short of playing money and she asked me if I would please be her partner and contribute $200 for a 50 percent interest while she played some "super" system of hers at the crap table. She said that with $400, the profit potential would be much more than twice what it would be with her own $200. That premise seemed plausible enough — and I was curious about her system, so I gave her $200.

We found places at a crap table and she promptly placed a $1 bet on something (I don't recall what). Just as promptly, I said, "Honey, I'd like to terminate our partnership, so please give me back my $200." My point was that with a $400 "bank" no system that made sense could begin with a bet so small.* Plusses and minuses, passes and misses, reds and blacks; they all tend to come in bunches much of the time — and because of that, a preponderance of one's winning sequences are always likely to come in the early stages of any system he happens to be using. A progression of any kind that starts with 1 is likely to have spent most of its momentum by the time it reaches any number of consequence. If it's one in which bets are raised as you lose, then there will be at least 50 percent more wins at the starting bet than at any other point in the series.

I tell you this story to point up a common illusion of those who attempt to devise winning progressions. They assume that what is needed is a maximum number of trials within a

---

*This was before I discovered that a Fibonacci series beginning with 1 could be made into a viable system (see page 75).

dollar limit determined by their own circumstances and temperament. If they're interested in a system that seems to require 10 consecutive bets in order to be virtually certain to win once, they will develop a 10-digit progression in which total risk and the biggest single bet are held within prescribed limits. To do this, they usually discover that their progression must begin with extremely small bets.

The fallacy of this approach is often compounded by the normal impulse to fashion a progressive series of bets in such a way that the big bets toward the end of the series produce proportionately bigger net profits. After all, it does seem inane to risk $100 in order to win $1 or $2.

The proper approach is to test any untried system against actual casino decisions or truly random numbers, so as to ascertain: (1) the expected win-loss ratios with bet series of different lengths; and (2) where in your bet series you are likely to get the major proportion of your wins. This last requirement is vital.

You will find that virtually all up-as-you-lose progressions designed for even chances, produce most of their wins in their early stages. That reflects the fact that repeat sequences of such chances occur every bit as frequently, if not more so, as alternating sequences. If you're using a progression and betting red in roulette when five consecutive reds come along, three or four of those winning bets will take place at the first number in your bet series. I hope I've made my point and that you can see how foolish it could be to use any even-chance progression in which first-number wins were of insignificant value.

With respect to the length of your progression, a somewhat similar principle applies. You may find that, given 18 consecutive chances, you would win 999 times out of 1000, but that 18 trials at progressively increased cost would involve totally unacceptable risk. Ten trials might give you a 50 to 1 win probability, so if your average win looked to be considerably larger than 1/50th of the total risk, that length might be feasible. But with a 10-stage progression, you would still have to risk sizeable sums in order to win "peanuts."

Now suppose you found that with a six-digit series, your win-loss ratio would be about 6 to 1, but that your total risk with such a series would be only about four and one-half times the average individual win. If the average win were $10, that would imply profits of $60 for each $45 you could expect to lose — a pretty fair profit margin. In that case it would seem that you had found a truly practical answer to your problem.

It just so happens that the last set of ratios mentioned applies to the parlay system to be discussed later in this chapter. This dissertation, however, is designed primarily to show you how I have approached the whole matter of workable progressions and to suggest to you how you might go about developing any ideas of your own along similar lines.

I must confess that my own conscious recognition of the relative importance of those first-number wins in a progression designed for even chances, came only after this book had been three-fourths completed — and after the laborious task of testing and tabulating results for the various systems had been 100 percent completed. Therefore, the test results you will see in this chapter are based on bet series that are not quite as good as they might be. You will be shown the series on which the tests were made, as well as improved versions of the same type of series.

One thing I wish to make absolutely clear is this: Even though I've had some rather extraordinary results with some of these systems, none of them are represented as "sure things." There is no "sure thing" in any game of chance. Although you are not about to receive the keys to the casino cashier's cage, you will be introduced to several systems that do seem to reverse the percentages, when and if they're properly used over a reasonable period of time.

Generically speaking, there are two kinds of "winning" systems: (1) one which when skillfully used over a reasonable time period usually wins on balance; and (2) one which may or may not win 50 percent of the time, or on balance, but which always has a realistic potential for exceptional profit relative to the amount of risk involved. Unless otherwise indicated, the systems discussed in this chapter meet one of those two criteria.

For progressions on even chances in which bets are increased to offset earlier losses, I usually advocate playing for two or more wins per series. This is the best means I know by which the rate of bet escalation can be kept within bounds without any impairment of profit potentials. The only exceptions to this general rule would be those short Martingale-type bet series that are good when one wants to bet that an abnormal sequence is about to end.

Examine the two bet series below. Since the parlay series is twice the length of the other series, its average number of wins per series loss should equal the other series' win-loss ratio. Its requirement of two consecutive wins at any point has been offset by doubling the number of chances. Each series will produce roughly equivalent profits at the points that correspond.

| PARLAY | $\frac{2}{6}$ | $\frac{2}{4}$ | $\frac{3}{5}$ | $\frac{4}{5}$ | $\frac{6}{7}$ | $\frac{8}{7}$ | $\frac{11}{8}$ | $\frac{15}{9}$ | $\frac{20}{9}$ | $\frac{27}{10}$ | Total Risk 98 |
| SERIES | | | | | | | | | | | Net Profit at each point |

| SINGLE-WIN | | | $\frac{5}{5}$ | $\frac{10}{5}$ | $\frac{22}{7}$ | $\frac{45}{8}$ | $\frac{91}{9}$ | Total Risk 173 |
| SERIES | | | | | | | | Net Profit at each point |

The superiority of the Parlay progression is obvious, is it not? Ergo, a properly constructed bet series using parlays or the double-win approach to be described shortly is the way to go if you plan to offset losses by increasing your bets on any even chance.

The money-management systems you are about to meet take practicality as well as effectiveness into account. As you review them, please bear in mind that the test results cited are based largely, if not entirely, upon casino dice decisions unless otherwise noted. I have definite reservations as to their applicability to the two-zero wheel in roulette.

THE PARLAY PROGRESSIONS

The nice thing about a successful parlay on an even-money bet is that it yields a profit three times as large as the amount originally risked. For that reason a progression using parlays can be effective without being as steep as it would otherwise have to be.

After much experimenting on paper and in the casinos, I have found that a series of six parlay attempts provides a satisfactory compromise between excessive commitment on a single series of bets, and excessive risk of losing series being bunched together.

The seven-number parlay series mentioned earlier in this book began with a small bet which was repeated but not parlayed until it lost. When it lost, you bet the next higher number in the series and tried for a parlay if you won that bet. If you missed the parlay, you repeated the process with the next five numbers until you made your parlay or lost the whole series. In either case, you went back to that first number in your series and started over.

Extensive tests with the following series showed an average expectancy of one series loss for each six successful parlays:

$$\frac{5}{5} \quad \frac{5}{10} \quad \frac{8}{14} \quad \frac{12}{18} \quad \frac{18}{24} \quad \frac{25}{27} \quad \frac{35}{32}$$ Total Risk 108
Net Profit at each point

In many instances with this series, we had almost as many first-number wins as the total number of successful parlays. Overall results were quite satisfactory, though they were by no means consistent. There were a few occasions when losses of three almost successive series occurred with as few as five or six intervening parlays. However, tested on about 3,000 casino dice decisions, the system showed a nice profit.

Against H.B. Adams' *3,240 Casts of the Dice*, equivalent to about 16 hours of casino play, the above series won $674, or almost $43 per hour, despite the loss of 19 bet series of $108 each. In that test I used the "Reverse/Repeat" method of bet selection, but in most of the testing, the opposite method — "Pattern" — proved superior.

Refer to the net profit figures in the above series and observe what happens when that first non-parlay bet is eliminated. Instead of: 10 14 18 24 27 32, those parlay profits become 15 19

23 29 32 37 — and suggest quite clearly that with no reduction in the number of parlay attempts, the shortened series should do as well or better than the original series. (All authorities seem to agree that in matters of chance, what happens before has no bearing on what happens afterward; the fact that those parlays in the tests were always preceded by one extra losing bet should have had no influence on the test results.)

Subsequent testing has convinced me that you'll get nearly 50 percent more wins at the first number in a series of this type than at any other number in the series. That being so, series built along the lines of the two immediately following should produce better results than the first series shown above.

A. $\quad \frac{7}{21} \quad \frac{8}{17} \quad \frac{10}{15} \quad \frac{13}{14} \quad \frac{18}{16} \quad \frac{25}{19} \quad$ Total Risk 81
Profit at each point in series

B. $\quad \frac{4}{12} \quad \frac{5}{11} \quad \frac{6}{9} \quad \frac{8}{9} \quad \frac{11}{10} \quad \frac{15}{11} \quad$ Total Risk 49
Profit at each point in series

These figures can be translated into quarters instead of dollars by those of you who might wish to experiment with minimum risk. As you know, there are many 25¢ crap tables in Nevada.

Another excellent way of reducing risk is to have a partner using the same system, but always betting opposite to you. If you do that, the only circumstance that could cause you both to lose at the same time would be a sequence of 12 alternating wins and losses; something that will not happen once in several thousand decisions either at craps or roulette.

Sometimes when I've lost my whole bet series, instead of simply starting over, I've tried three more parlays somewhat larger in amount than the first three numbers in my regular series. This would be a temporizing move designed to take some of the "sting" out of that series loss. For example, if I'd lost the above mentioned "A" series, I might try for one parlay in this series:

AMOUNT OF BET	10	15	20
NET PROFIT	30	35	35

With this short series, *used only as a supplement*, my win-loss record has been better than 2 to 1; in other words, it has netted about $75 for each loss of $45.

The major problem with a six-number parlay is the considerable risk of three, four, or more series losses occurring close together. That risk can be partially overcome by partners betting opposite to each other, or by a single player betting as if he had a partner. To do this he would make just one bet on each spin or come-out — and that bet would be the net difference between the two bets a partnership would be making if he had a partner. His bet, of course, would be on the side scheduled to make the larger of the two bets at any given point.

Assume for example, that your series is 5 10 15 20 25 35. You are playing roulette and red wins the first two bets, while black loses them. Since the hypothetical partners both have bet the same amounts, no actual bets are made at all — and no money changes hands. Now black is due to bet 15 while red goes back to 5, so you would bet the difference, 10 on black. If you win that bet, your next bet on black would be 30, while red's next bet would be 10, so your next single bet would be 20 on black. With a bit of practice you'll find that it is not too difficult to do the required calculating in time to get your money down for the next throw or spin.

A nine-number parlay series greatly reduces the risk of bunched series losses. Tests using my pet bet-selection procedure produced an average of more than 17 parlays for each lost series. I have a friend who likes craps and whose modus operandi is exactly what I've described in the preceding paragraph, except that he uses the longer bet series. His single bet on each come-out is the difference between the amounts he and his imaginary partner would have bet. His success record is astonishing. If it's not 100 percent, it is very nearly that on the basis of profit or loss figures for each of about 20 trips to Las Vegas. Here is the parlay series he generally uses:

5	10	15	20	25	35	50	75	100	Total of all bets — $335
15	25	30	30	25	30	40	65	75	Net profit at each point

He likes to find an uncrowded table where the action is

speeded up, and there he bets both sides exactly as if he had a partner who was betting don't, while he was betting pass. If he can't find such a table, he looks for one where there is a lot of player enthusiasm, and there he will play the pass line only.

The above series is excellent, but I suspect that it might yield slightly improved results long range, if it were modified as follows:

$\frac{8}{24}$	$\frac{11}{25}$	$\frac{15}{26}$	$\frac{20}{26}$	$\frac{27}{27}$	$\frac{37}{30}$	$\frac{50}{32}$	$\frac{70}{42}$	$\frac{100}{62}$	Total of all bets — $338
									Net profit at each point

In the second series, you can see that the average parlay profit should amount to at least 27. Twelve wins at $27 each would yield $324, while 17 wins would yield $459, or $121 more than the risk represented by the entire series.

Actually, using the pseudo-partnership procedure as outlined above, the real risk in either of the above series would have to be about $55 less than the sum of all bets, for if one side were to lose nine successive parlay attempts, the other side would be virtually certain to make at least two parlays.

For anyone more interested in consistent winnings than in fast action with a terrific risk reward potential, the parlay series is highly recommended. It is one of the best.

THE DOUBLE-WIN PROGRESSIONS

The procedure here is almost identical to that used with the parlays. However, this type of progression is more conservative and perhaps a more reliable performer.

At each point in a bet series of from five to eight numbers, you play for two consecutive wins, but after one win you repeat the same bet instead of leaving your winnings on the table as you do with parlays. This means that when you have a win followed by a loss, you are even; you haven't won or lost that bet, so you repeat it and keep repeating it until you either lose that number or win it twice. As with the parlays, when you have a double win at any point — or when you reach the end of your series without any wins — you start over at the first number in the series.

With these progressions, the predominance of wins in the early stages of a series is more pronounced than it is with parlay series, in which that predominance applies mainly to the first bet in a series. In a double-win series you'll have a progressively declining number of wins as you move up through the series. This fact was not taken fully into account when I first began to use and test these progressions. Since the test results and my casino experience were both quite favorable, I am very optimistic about the results anticipated from the improved bet series to be described and discussed a bit later.

Originally I found that a nine-digit double-win series in which the first small bet was repeated until it lost, before moving up the series — no double win required — would show an average of 60 or more plusses for each loss of a series; whereas the total risk involved had to be no more than 35 to 40 times the average profit on each win. That meant that normally you would lose your whole bet series only once in a typical five-hour session, and that your average margin of profit over loss would be close to 33 percent.

Here is the type of bet series I've subjected to very extensive testing and used profitably in casinos:

$\frac{2}{2}$	$\frac{5}{8}$	$\frac{7}{7}$	$\frac{10}{6}$	$\frac{15}{6}$	$\frac{23}{7}$	$\frac{35}{8}$	$\frac{53}{9}$	$\frac{80}{10}$	Total Risk 230
									Net Profit at each point

Due to the very large number of $2 profits, the average win with this series would be only $5 or $6. Now let's see how the same series would look if we eliminated that initial $2 bet:

$\frac{5}{10}$	$\frac{7}{9}$	$\frac{10}{8}$	$\frac{15}{8}$	$\frac{23}{9}$	$\frac{35}{10}$	$\frac{53}{11}$	$\frac{80}{12}$	Risk 228
								Net Profit at each point

The average profit in the revised series will be more than $9, while the win-loss ratio should be no worse than 40 to 1. Actually, on the basis of mathematical logic, as well as the 60 to 1 ratio achieved by the nine-digit series, this ratio for the revised series should be 45 to 1. Thus, I estimate that the second series above should win between $360 and $405 for each loss of $228.

Having a strong personal aversion to large bets that can win only very small sums, I have seldom gone beyond the sixth bet in this type of series. Sometimes I attempt to ease out of my predicament by repeating my last losing bet and if I win, by then trying for a parlay. At other times I've accepted my loss and then have backed up only three or four numbers in my series, instead of going all the way back to the smallest bet. For example, if I lost 35 in the above series, I might go back to the 10 and continue trying for double wins from that point. In that way I would recoup $20 or more of my $95 loss on the series if I won one of my next four bets.

Betting opposites with a partner, he would have to have four double wins if you were to lose your whole series. That would, of course, materially reduce risk. A team of two using the system properly for any reasonable period should win fairly consistently, with one proviso: I am convinced that a major element in their success would be their adherence to my preferred methods of bet selection (Chapter 2).

On a team basis, satisfactory results would undoubtedly be obtained with a shortened series such as:

$$\frac{5}{10} \quad \frac{7}{9} \quad \frac{10}{8} \quad \frac{15}{8} \quad \frac{23}{9} \quad \frac{35}{10} \quad \text{Risk 95}$$
Net Profit at each point

Net risk for partners on this series would be $65 (or 65 quarters) while their average win would be about $9 (or 9 quarters). The win-loss ratio should approximate 12 to 1. This shorter series would also be a fairly sound venture for an individual, but he'd have to be aware of the heightened risk of bunched series losses. The minimum series for a team or an individual should never contain less than five increasing bets.

We have dwelled at length on this system's strong points and its virtues. Perhaps it is time to take a brief look at "the other side of the coin." I have a little booklet which purports to tabulate 12,500 actual dice rolls in leading Nevada casinos. That would represent close to 70 hours of play. Using an eight-digit double-win series with an average win of about $8 and series risk of $209, I checked results *with one partner betting pass and the other, don't pass.*

The results were not good. The passing partner wound up with a profit of $675, but his opposite number had a loss of $362. So the partners' net gain was only $313, little more than $2 per hour for each of them. I have no way of knowing whether those dice decisions were authentic as claimed, but some of the data derived from the tests was significant.

About one-third of all winning bets in this test, 418 out of 1,267, occurred at the first bet in the series. The second bet accounted for 289 wins. So those first two smallest numbers in the series produced 56 percent of all the double wins. This ratio appears to be pretty typical and clearly demonstrates why the profit figures on those first two bets in progressions of this type are so very important.

Whether the disappointing overall results of this test reflect upon the reliability of my own experience and previous testing as a barometer of what this system will do, I can't say with certainty, but I strongly doubt it. I believe those results point up the superiority of my own method of bet selection. On the poorest facing pages in the little book, there were three series losses and 28 profits, producing a net loss of $403. When I used my Pattern and Reverse/Repeat methods on the same pages, I came up with two series losses and 26 double wins for a net loss of $210 — a considerable improvement. This, of course, proved nothing, but it was at least suggestive. Incidentally, the booklet in question was published in Santa Barbara, California in the '50s and is entitled *Play To Win.*

At the risk of boring you with the specifics of more testing, I will tell you that when the original nine-number series with the $6 average profit was tried on Adams' 3,240 *Casts of the Dice* it yielded a net profit of about $1,000, equivalent to about $30 per hour for each of the partners.

An individual's stake for this system should be at least double the risk represented by his bet series, and triple that risk if his series has less than eight bets. However, partners working together can get by with less. Too thin a margin is not recommended for this or any other gambling game.

THE KEY SYSTEM

This is a good partnership system, but for one person it has a less attractive risk-reward factor than the two progressions previously described. It differs from them in two major respects. The first bet in this one *is* repeated until it loses; and when you win one of the succeeding bets, instead of trying for a parlay or double win of that bet, you must usually win two smaller bets before you've won your series and are ready to begin a new one.

In the examples below, the numbers in the top row are called "prime" numbers. When you lose one of these, you advance to the next higher prime number. When you win a prime number, you go to the smaller number directly beneath it, and if you win that one, you go to the bottom number in the column. When you lose one of those bets in the vertical column, you go back up the column. As you can see, when you back and fill in any column, you will be accumulating small profits. To win most vertical columns, you must win three times consecutively or four out of five, five out of seven, or six out of nine bets. When you've won all the numbers in any vertical column, you have won that series and you start over.

Here are two sample "Key" progressions:

A. PRIME NUMBERS	10	15	16	20	30	40	50	Risk 181; Part-
		8	11	15	20	30	45	ners' risk 111
			7	11	15	25	40	

B. PRIME NUMBERS	2	3	5	7	10	15	20	Risk 62; Part-
		3	3	5	7	11	15	ners' risk 48
			2	3	4	7	11	

In series A above, if you lost your first two bets, your next bet would be 16. If you won that one, you'd then bet 11 and if you won that, 7 would be your next bet. If you lost the 7, you'd go back up the same column and bet 11 again. In other words, you go down the vertical columns as you win and up them as you lose. Whenever you lose a prime number you move to the next higher prime number. When you win any vertical column or lose the last prime number, you go back to the first bet in your series.

I have tested this system, using series A above, on 780 casino dice decisions picked at random — about 15 hours of play. The results were surprising; plus $2,034 equivalent to $135 per hour for the partnership. Granted that 780 decisions are far too few to be considered conclusive, and the figures did not take come-out 12's into account, nevertheless they were so impressive that one of my objectives of the moment is to find a partner who will take the trouble to master the thing so that we can put it to the acid test in Nevada.

Incidentally, you may find, as I have, that finding such a partner is no small project. My first volunteer, a bright young stockbroker who knew craps, went over to Vegas with me, and after 10 harrowing minutes, threw in the towel. He simply could not keep track of what he was supposed to do. The "Pattern" system of bet selection proved more difficult for him than remembering the numbers in our bet series.

As a further test of the thing, I hand-picked a short series of 36 decisions in which one partner would have won only 12 bets while losing twice that many. Again, the outcome was less unfavorable than I had anticipated. The losing partner lost $163, while his opposite number showed a profit of $131.

However, this system can, and often does, take one rapidly to the higher numbers of his bet series. That is its main drawback for individual play, and also why the partners' bankrolls should be about $500 each if they intend to utilize series A or the equivalent. If they stand next to each other and exchange chips as needed, their requirement might be cut to about $300 each.

THE FIBONACCI SYSTEM

I don't know who Mr. Fibonacci was, or why, long ago his name was given to a rather ordinary series of numbers. In a

Fibonacci series each number equals the sum of the two preceding numbers. Thus,

    1 2 3 5 8 13 21 34 55 89 144 233   Risk 608

is the series you'll use for this system (unless you decide to shorten the series).

Among the systems that I like, this one is unique in two particulars:

1. One could use it eight hours per day for a solid week with reasonable expectation of winning about $20 per hour and having not a single serious loss. A husband and wife team betting opposites could anticipate $40 per hour profit.
2. Though the chance of serious loss is very small, the risk as related to the rate of probable gain is large. One loss of a full bet series would wipe out 30 hours of profit.

You start with the smallest number and move up one notch each time you lose. When you win a bet, you back up one notch — and whenever you win two successive bets, or two out of three (+ − +), you end that series and start a new one. Simple, isn't it? It is completely mechanical, with no guesswork or judgment factor — but as is often the case with a newly discovered gold mine, there is a "hitch."

This system may still be being sold at $100 a copy by direct mail, as it was several years ago, with instructions to use it at craps betting *don't pass*. I have tested it against 8,000 dice decisions, equivalent to 132 hours of play, and found that betting pass or don't pass, one should expect one lost series in every 1,600 decisions (26.7 hours at 60 decisions per hour). At that rate he would show a net loss of about $40 for his 27 hours of effort.

However, based on the same 8,000 decisions, if a player had switched from pass to don't using either of my two preferred bet-selection procedures, his results would have been startlingly different. In one instance, he would have lost his full series exactly *once*; in the other, he would have had just *two* such losses. A partnership using both procedures and betting opposites would have experienced a total of three series losses amounting to $1,368 while winning approximately $5,280 for a net gain of $3,912 — not bad tax-free pay for three weeks of hard labor even in these days of the shrinking dollar.

Past performance, of course, is no guarantee of future results. I can tell you, however, that the consistent disparity between results using the switching procedures as opposed to betting either pass or don't, was impressive enough to convince me that it will hold up. If one were to use this system for three to five hours at *craps, baccarat,* or *single-zero roulette,* the odds that he'd never lose his bet series would be enormous — surely better than 5 to 1.

I have used the system at a Las Vegas crap table only once. In a three-hour session of 168 decisions I won $58, losing 85 bets and winning 83. My biggest bet in the session was $34, and that figure was reached once.

The system appears to be ideal for team play; one partner using what I call the "Pattern" method of bet selection, the other using "Reverse-Repeat."

I have seldom recommended systems involving substantial risk in return for small gain. This is an exception only because the risk of any loss in a single session is so very small. Furthermore, it is distinctly possible that one could end his bet series with the tenth number (89) and still have an adequate margin of safety. If he did that, his whole bet series would represent $231 and he could play with a starting bankroll of about $300. This shortened series has not been thoroughly tested and is suggested merely as a relevant "idea" rather than as a recommendation.

For those of you who may wish to try this system at a $5-minimum table, that might be done as follows:

First you would familiarize yourself with the whole series — at least that part of it from $5 to $233. In your own "special" series, the first six bets would be 6 5 6 5 6 5. Beyond those numbers the Fibonacci numbers would begin with 21, and when you were beyond those first six bets you would adhere to the rules of ending any series after two successive or two out of three wins, and backing up after any single win.

While betting the 5s and 6s, you start over when you win any one of the first four bets.

If you win only your fifth bet in that beginning series, your next bet is 8 as in the "regular" series, and you continue as in the regular series. If you lose the 8, next bet is 13. If you win 13, you've won two of the last three bets, and the series is ended. If you had won the 8, that would have ended the series.

If you win only your sixth bet, next bet is 13 and you continue with the regular series as above.

If you lose your first six bets, your next bet is 21 in the "regular" series and you continue as above.

I've experimented with this $5 minimum procedure enough to feel reasonably confident that it will yield results quite similar to, if not slightly superior to, the results obtained when starting at 1.

BET SELECTION

As indicated above, this is *vital*. Take your choice of one of these two procedures:

1. Each bet the *opposite* of the *second* preceding decision (preferred).
2. Each bet the *same* as the *second* preceding decision.

If you then seem to persistently lose more bets than you win, you may have made the wrong choice. In that case you may switch to the opposite procedure, *but do not switch while you're in the middle of any bet series.*

To keep track of that second preceding decision, you should rack or stack your chips of two differing denominations in the same order as the last few decisions; *i.e.,* red chips for passes, white chips for misses.

THE SUPER MARTINGALE SYSTEM

As you know, the odds against a specific even chance coming up six times in succession are 63 to 1. Theoretically, if you wished to bet against such an occurrence, you would have to risk $63 in order to win $1. However, you are about to be introduced to a practical procedure that will enable you to bet against six repeats of anything without risking more than 15 times the amount of your average win — and without forcing you to skip two or more decisions while waiting for a specific betting situation.

If you decide to use this system your first step might be to walk up to a crap or roulette table and bet just $1 that the first decision you see will not repeat itself. If you lose that bet you will then begin to play more seriously. You will then have seen two passes or two reds, or whatever — and you will plan to bet in succession $5, $10, $20, and $40 that one of the next four decisions will not be a repeat of that same even chance.

When you win any one of those four bets, your net profit on the series will be $5 and you start over with the $5 bet. If you had won that original $1 bet, that would have meant that the last decision had alternated. You need two alternating decisions or a pair of repeats before you go into action, so you wait out the next decision, which must give you one or the other.

After two alternating decisions you will use the same Martingale series to bet that one of the following four decisions will be a repeat. Of course, whenever you win that bet you will have had two repeats, so you won't have to skip a decision; you simply bet that the next decision will reverse, and so on.

To clarify the above, if the last two decisions were:

A. + + or − − Bet that one of the next four decisions will reverse.
B. + − or − + Skip the next decision, and if it alternates again, bet that one of the following four decisions will repeat. If that skipped decision was a repeat, bet as in A above.

Doing this, you will average very close to two wins for every five decisions, and you should lose your bet series about once in 20 or more decisions on average.

If, as the books tell you, "dice have no memories," the procedure as outlined should give you no perceptible advantage. Conversely, if indeed there is a "law of diminishing probability," as I firmly believe, you will find that this simple little system wins on balance — though, admittedly, it is a bit of a "grind."

I concede, of course, that when we've already had two specific occurrences, the odds are no longer 63 to 1 that they won't be followed by four more like occurrences. I don't know what those odds really are — nor does anyone else — but believe me, they are better than 15 to 1. On the basis of my own experience plus tests covering thousands of dice decisions, I have no hesitancy in estimating those odds to be closer to 20 to 1.

Using $5 units, one should average close to $100 in winnings for each loss of his $75 bet series. That translates into $20 to $30 per hour with what appears to be minimum risk.

In my own play I have seldom used a straight Martingale. Instead, I've used one of the following Grand Martingale series:

5 15 35 75   (or)   5 12 25 50

and I believe they have produced results that are somewhat superior in terms of the sums at risk. No matter which four-stage bet series you use, you will find this to be a most reliable system when used over a reasonable period. Short range, however, there is the usual risk of bunched series losses. I suggest table switching as the best antidote for that, since loss of one's bet series often suggests a trend away from "choppy" results, to long sequences. Your starting bankroll should be about 3 to 4 times the risk represented by all the bets in your series.

Using this same system more conservatively, one might further reduce his chance of loss by beginning each bet series only after three consecutive repeats or three successive alternating decisions. To keep track he would have to rack or stack his chips of two different colors in the same order as the last few decisions — and there would be many instances when he'd make no bet at all. However, doing this should not materially impair his profit potential.

In my own records of Las Vegas dice results there are two sessions of about 300 decisions each, where the system, as initially described, would have done quite poorly. In one session it would have lost $160, while in the other it would have had a $35 profit. In contrast to those dismal figures, this more "conservative" procedure would have netted $265 in those same 600 decisions. It would have won 113 bets while losing its $75 bet series just four times.

For one who feels that he *must* win, and who can risk $100 or so, there are few safer procedures in any casino than this.

Equally relevant from a purely personal standpoint is the fact that the success I've enjoyed with the system seems to prove beyond reasonable doubt the validity of my own pet theory of "diminishing probability." If you try it I am sure that you'll agree.

This is a good system for a $50 budget. Starting with 1 2 5 10 as his or her bet series, average profit in excess of $5 per hour would be a reasonable expectation. Then with $20 of accumulated profit he or she might double the hourly profit potential by changing the bet series to 2 4 8 16 or 2 4 8 15.

THE 2-5 SYSTEM

One of the best systems I know is also one of the simplest, and it exemplifies the inherent advantage of pulling back after winning bets. It is a five-number bet series designed so that most combinations of two wins in the series will yield a fair profit relative to total risk. For example:

5 7 12 15 25 (risk 64) *or* 2 3 5 7 10 (risk 27)

With these series you start with the low number and move up until you have two wins, or until you win or lose the last number in your series. In either case you simply repeat the process. Actually, this is nothing but a radically modified version of what in my first chapter I called the "Foolproof System." This version, when used by partners betting opposite each other, may not be foolproof, but it comes close. Tested on over 3,000 casino dice decisions — about 60 hours of play — each partner's average hourly gain equalled about one-third of the total risk represented by his series of five bets, and there were only four five-hour sessions during which the partnership showed modest net losses.

An individual can expect to grind out decent winnings if his luck is about average — and if he plays for a reasonable period. He will get his two wins about 84 percent of the time, and about half those wins will come before he reaches the fourth bet in his series. In the above two sample series, profits on any two wins in the first three bets would amount to just less than one-fifth of the total risk, a respectable ratio. When using the system without a partner, my own bet-selection method has generally been the "Pattern" described in Chapter 2.

Partners betting opposite will seldom be called upon to bet the same amounts at the same time, but when that does happen, their bets can be "imaginary" until one partner has two imaginary wins. At that point he'll go back to the first number in the series, while the other partner continues the series from the point where the imaginary bets ceased.

On several occasions I have played this system with a lady partner who objected to the idea of betting opposites — so we bet the same way. Here is the way we did it. Whenever the system required us to bet the same amount, she would hold off until I had had either three losses or one win, whichever came first. At that point she would begin her own series, making the same bets I made, but in different amounts. This procedure worked fairly well. We used a series that totaled 54 or 55 and, as I recall, we not only showed an overall profit, but in one four-hour session, our best, we managed to win just less than $400 — $195 apiece.

You might try this same system with only four numbers in your bet series. This has not been subjected to serious testing by me, but I suspect that a series such as 5-6-8-12, with its mild upward bias, would prove nearly as effective as a five-number series, *especially for partners betting opposites*. It would be less practical for one player due to the risk of bunched series losses.

Incidentally, Table 2 on page 41 reveals the rather surprising fact that the probability of making at least two correct calls in four tries on any even chance is better than 2 to 1. Perhaps you'd like to even the score with someone who has taken your money. If so, offer him 3 to 2 odds on this proposition. If he falls for it, you'll take his money all day long.

Thus far we've looked mainly at progressions in which bets are raised primarily to recoup earlier losses. It is time now to consider the opposite approach; namely, escalation of winning bets only.

STRAIGHT-UP SYSTEM

I would guess that at least 80 percent of all professional gamblers advocate escalation of winning bets only. There is no question but that this procedure enables one to win more, with less risk, than the opposite approach. There is definite question, however, as to whether it enables one to win as frequently as the other approach.

This type of progressive betting can be frustrating. After a a series of small losses you finally get a run of winning bets. Your problem then becomes one of deciding whether to cut back; and at what point to do so. If you play your luck to the hilt, you'll lose your biggest bet. You know that if you keep on, one or two additional losses of that size will wipe out all your profit. On the other hand, if you pull out or arbitrarily reduce your bets, you may miss a substantial portion of the profit that might have been yours.

There is no easy solution to this problem, but my experience has just about convinced me that if I habitually stop or pull way back at what seems to be a sensible point in a winning sequence, my chance of winding up a winner will be considerably better than if I wait for losses before retreating. Remember that poor fellow who left $22,000 on the table!

A sales manager for a computer company near Los Angeles likes to shoot craps. He visits Las Vegas on a majority of his weekends and usually confines his play to "line" bets — pass and don't pass — seldom taking or laying the odds. He escalates when winning and almost always bets that the next decision will be the reverse of the previous decision. If he loses two or three times in a row, he stops betting until after the next reversal.

This gentleman insists that in 1977 he made about $7,000 sticking to one simple system and almost always using the following progression — a sort of modified Ascot:

6   6   12   18   30   45   60   90   120   150   200

Starting with $6 he does not bet the 12 until he's won two successive 6s. Then if he loses 12 twice, he goes back to 6. If he wins 12 either at his first try or second, he's on his way. From that point, each time he wins a bet he moves up one notch in his series and when he loses, he repeats the losing bet until he has two losses or a net profit at that level, whichever happens first. If he loses twice, he starts a new series. When he reaches 200, he makes just one bet, win or lose, and then repeats the whole process.

I cannot vouch for the accuracy of his claimed 1977 winnings, but I can tell you that the man in question is a solid citizen, the sort of person one would be inclined to believe. I believe that my description of his system is accurate, for I've watched him closely on several occasions.

If you're a realist, you know that you have to count on losing about as many bets as you'll win. If you plan to escalate as you win, your problem is how to scale your bets so as to maximize profit potential without unduly increasing risk. The big factor in your favor is the likelihood that many of your winning bets will come in bunches instead of alternating with losing bets.

I believe the betting system described above is a good one. The 5 5 7 10 15 22 30 progression mentioned earlier is also good, but it may be too conservative for many of you. Another sound and quite popular way of escalating more rapidly is to parlay the first bet in your planned series.

Suppose you plan to parlay your minimum bet and your stake is $150 to $200. Your small bet will probably be $5, and if you win a series of five bets scaled 5 10 15 25 40, your $95 profit may justify anything from a 30 percent to a 50 percent increase in the size of your following bets. Of course, any increase should be geared to the net increase in your bankroll. With this type of progression, when you begin play your small bet should be no more than one-thirtieth of your stake, but as you win, that ratio can be larger as long as you have a cushion of profit. Note that with this last bet series, you draw down $5 after your second win, another $5 after your third win, and $10 after the fourth win, so that you'll be even or better if you lose at any point after that initial parlay.

The real problem with a steep bet series of this type has to do with one's action when he loses the fourth bet or one farther along than that in his series. A conservative player would go all the way back and start a new series, while an optimist might cut back just enough so that if he lost his next bet, he'd still be at least even on that series. Unless one wished to "go for broke," it would make no sense to risk a net loss on a series that had begun with four or more consecutive winning bets.

You may have observed that this type of bet escalation is especially suitable for craps where the odds on pass-line bets can materially enhance profitability. It is also adaptable to roulette — even with 2-zero wheels, but it is definitely inappropriate for blackjack.

One final comment that applies to any up-as-you-win system: *it is not necessary and may even be inadvisable to use either of my preferred bet-selection methods.* You're hoping for a long sequence of unbalanced decisions, so continuous betting on the same even chance is as good a way as any to get that sequence. I have sometimes imagined that playing for alternating runs of three — three passes followed by three don'ts; then three passes, etc., might increase the probability of extremely unbalanced results, but I have no statistical evidence of that.

THE STEP LADDER

This is one of the most interesting money-management systems I know; and one of the more effective. If one is patient enough and not too greedy, he need not lose very often with it.

It can be used on the even chances in craps, roulette and even baccarat. Success with it depends on the certainty that sooner or later one or the other of those even chances will get the upper hand and win a good deal more often than its normal 50 percent quota.

Even-chance sequences of 5 repeats, or 7 out of 10, or 25 out of 40 are just as inevitable as death and taxes — and when such sequences occur, the user of this system is likely to be profiting handsomely. Here is the way it works:

I use an arbitrary bet series, each ascending number of which I like to think of as a rung of a ladder. I want to climb that ladder one rung at a time, and to do so safely, the rungs must not be too far apart; at least, not until my upward climb has gathered momentum. The following bet series is one that I've found to be practical:

1 2 3 4 (5) 6 7 8 10 12 14 16 18 20 22 25 30 35 40 45
            50 60 70 85 100 115 130 150 170 200 250 300 etc.

With this series your first bet should be 5, and you move up one rung when you win and down one when you lose. Thus, if wins and losses alternate or balance out, you're going to lose $1 for each two decisions. If they alternated 30 times, you'd be out $15, which could be boring. If they didn't alternate or balance out, you might have your chips on the wrong "horse" and that also could be boring. The first of those eventualities is highly unlikely, and the second one can be eliminated by betting on both horses in this two-horse race.

You bet both pass and don't pass (or) red and black to start with. If you wish to avoid the embarrassment of doing something so patently ridiculous, you might just calculate the difference between the two bets called for and make the single bet representing that difference. Betting both "horses" in this way eliminates much of the risk of long waits before your own horse starts to move.

Assume that your first bet is 5 in the above series. (If you're betting both ways, or have a partner, that (5) bet can be skipped and your two bets could then be 6 and 5.) In any case it should not be long before one side or the other wins the 8 bet. At that point the winner will have won more than the loser has lost and the loser will retire. From then on, it will be a one-horse race for which there are no hard and fast rules.

If you use a single stack of chips or just one of the racks at the dice table for all your bets in any one series, you'll always know about how you stand on that series and you can be guided accordingly. I like to move up one rung each time I break even or am a net winner at any "rung" of my ladder. When I lose one bet, I repeat at the same level. If I lose two bets at the same level, I may repeat depending upon my frame of mind and the state of my bankroll at the moment. Thus, if wins and losses alternate, it is possible to move well into the higher numbers without having a substantial cushion of profit.

With two losses at the 10 or 12 level in the above series, I'd probably start over if my profit on that series had been entirely eliminated. Beyond the 12 level, one's profit could be adequate to justify a third try at any level where he had already sustained two losses. This, of course, assumes his willingness to risk a small loss in return for a chance to make a very large profit.

As I'm sure you know by this time, I have a strong personal inclination to stop on winning bets. I do not recall ever having taken more than one loss when I've been beyond the 20 level in a series such as the above. However, another player who did not feel as strongly as I do about protecting profits, might occasionally run this type of progression right up to the house limit where, of course, his profit could be enormous. In casino play my longest run to date with this same bet series took me to the 40 level — and a profit of more than $200.

An ultra-conservative method of play would be to move ahead in the series only when you are a net winner at any given level. If you lost and won the same amount, you'd have to win again before moving up; a net of three or more losses at any level would terminate that particular series.

The application of this system to the following hand-picked examples of actual casino dice decisions may prove instructive and helpful. (P=pass; D=don't pass)

	P	P	P	P	D	P	D	P	P	P
You	5	6	7	8	-10	10	-12	12	14	16
	P	D	P	P	D	P	P	P	D	P
	18	-20	20	22	-25	25	30	35	-40	40
	P	D	P	P	D	P				
	45	-50	50	60	-70	70	(Net: +266)			
PARTNER	-5	-4	-3	-2	(Net: -14)					

That sequence was followed by this one:

	D	D	P	D	P	D	P	D	D	D
You	5	6	-7	6	-7	6	-7	6	7	8
	P	D	D	D	D	P	D	D		
	-10	10	12	14	16	-18	18	20	(Net: +85)	
PARTNER	-5	-4	3	-4	3	-4	3	-4	-3	-2
	(Net: -18)									

When you look at that top sequence, which netted $252, it is hard to escape the conclusion that keeping on until you have three losses at any level could be foolhardy. That procedure would have converted a decent profit into a sizeable loss. The more prudent course might be to limit yourself to a net loss of two bets on any single rung of the ladder (or) to limit any continuing bet after two losses to an amount equal to, or less than your profit at that point.

In that same top sequence, if we had used the procedure described above as "ultra conservative," net profit would have been 149 and our last and biggest bet would have been 30. The loss of three 30s would have left us with a profit. Maybe those words "ultra conservative" should be changed to "prudent."

In any case, this system has a great deal of merit. In fact, some of its characteristics are similar to those that enabled Norman Leigh and his cohorts to "break the bank" in London and Nice, France with their reverse Labouchere. With "Step Ladder" a team might be helpful playing the even chances in roulette but not nearly as essential as it was with reverse Labouchere.

NOTE: Readers who contemplate using any of these systems on a partnership basis are urged to read my comments labeled "The Partnership Concept" on page 207 before attempting team play in any casino.

CHAPTER 7

Systems for Midget Bankrolls

This chapter is a follow-up on the suggestions made earlier for the benefit of vacationers and others who prefer not to risk serious money. They will have much more fun and an infinitely better chance to win if, rather than playing Keno and the slots, etc., they use conservative systems such as those mentioned in this and other chapters, playing any one of the three major casino games.

Here are a few variations of systems previously described, which can be used on the even-money bets in craps and roulette (and also in blackjack, but with somewhat greater risk).

MINI-VERSION OF THE "2-5" SYSTEM

At the beginning of this book I described a system that I said was virtually sure to win the long run when applied to any even or near-even proposition. It was a simple arithmetical progression in which bets kept increasing until profits overtook losses. I stated that it was impractical for use in these games, and so it is. But let's consider a drastically modified version of it, tailored to fit a $50 bankroll.

A.　1　2　3　4　5　　(risk: $15)
B.　2　3　5　7　10　　(risk: $27)

Start with 1 in series A, moving up the series, win or lose, until you have two wins or have completed the series. Then start over and do the same thing, continuing until you have a net loss of $15, or until at some point you lose $15 without any intervening profit. Suppose, for example, you have a few small gains; then on one sequence you win only the 2. You have lost $11. Now you bet 1, 2, and 3 and lose $6 more. Your unbroken loss at this point is $17 and it's time to go to series B.

Series B is played exactly the same way as series A, and you don't return to the first series until you have won at least $5 more than that $17 loss which caused you to change from one series to the other, I believe you'll be rather surprised at how well this little system performs, even if your batting average is unimpressive.

MINI-VERSION OF D'ALENBERT

This is the system in which bets are increased one unit when you lose and decreased one unit when you win. It can be rough if carried too far, but here's a way to cut risk sharply and still enjoy knowing that most of your winning bets are going to be larger than your losers. Use a series like the following:

1 2 3 ④ 5 6 7

With this one, your first bet would be the 4. If you win, go back to 3; if you lose go up to 5, and so forth. Whenever you lose the 7, your next bet should be the 4. Simple, isn't it? The nice thing is that you don't have to be terribly lucky to win with it.

THE PARLAY PROGRESSION

You may wish to refresh your memory on this one by referring to the description in the preceding chapter. It involves a bit more risk than the two mini-systems above, but the difference is slight and the profit potential may be superior. Here are suggested bet series:

A.		2	3	4	5	7	10	(31)
Profit if Won		6	7	7	6	7	9	

B.		4	5	8	(17)
Profit if Won		12	11	15	

If you lose the "A" series, you have a choice of either repeating it or continuing with the supplementary "B" series. Winning with the "B" series will cut your loss in half; and my experience with it suggests that it will win more than twice for each loss *when used as a supplement to the longer series*. The six-number series should average about six wins for each loss of the entire series. Remember to start a new series whenever you get a successful parlay; also to use one of the bet-selection methods described in Chapter 2.

THE REVERSE STEPLADDER

Here's one for a person who really doesn't like to gamble and just hates to lose; possibly your wife:

	1	1	1	1	1	1	1	1
$'s	2	2	2	2	2			
	5	5	5	5	5			

If she would be tickled to win $5 to $10 in an hour, this system is good for blackjack, as well as the even chances in craps and roulette. Give her $42 and tell her to pick her favorite game and to buy five $5 chips and seventeen $1 chips. She is then to make a separate stack of seven $1 chips.

She starts by betting $1 at a time, placing her net winnings with the bulk of her chips so that her stack of seven chips is never larger than that. Losses come off that stack, and whenever it has less than seven chips, winnings are added to it until it gets back to its starting point of seven chips. If she loses all seven of those chips, she then makes a stack of ten $1 chips and begins to bet $2 at a clip. When she has built that stack of 10 chips up to 18 chips, she resumes betting $1 with her stack of seven chips, just as she did when she started.

If your lady loses her second-round stack of 10 chips, she then intrepidly (or doggedly) moves up to the next level. She now bets $5 until she is $15 ahead, at which point she will resume betting $2 with a stack of ten $1 chips just as before. If perchance, she loses all her $5 chips — too bad, but as I've already indicated, that won't happen very often. As a matter of fact, playing this way she will reach that $5 betting level only on rare occasions.

You will note that what little risk there is in the above procedure could be still further reduced if at the beginning, one were simply to bet $1 until he or she had a net loss of $7. Then, if that point were ever reached, $2 bets would be in order, and so on.

I would suggest that with each of these systems, especially the first and third ones in this chapter, your strategy includes plans to raise the level of your bets modestly whenever your winnings approximate 50 percent of the amount originally risked. I'm sure you'll have no trouble fashioning bet series as good or better than those suggested here. So good luck!

The "Step Ladder" system (page 86) can be used with a very small stake. However, it was not included originally in this group of low-budget systems because it is somewhat involved. If attempted with a stake of $50 or less, I suggest a starting bet of $3 with a bet series beginning 12③45681012, etc. The losing side should stop when the other side wins the $6 bet. Using the system this way, I have won $150 in less than two hours, starting with a $40 bankroll.

These low-budget systems are representative, but by no means inclusive. There must be a dozen others described in this book. To name a few of these: the "Treadmill" system for craps, page 119; the small progressions on the 2 to 1 "sleepers" in roulette, page 145; and a modified Martingale series such as 2 2 6, for the even chances in craps and roulette, page 55.

CHAPTER 8

Craps

More fortunes are won and lost in this game than in all other casino games combined. At least that is true on this side of the Atlantic. Craps is played with dice on a felt-covered table usually about one and one-half times the size of a standard billiard table. The variety of bets it offers is just about limitless, and in some of these bets the house percentage can be as low as 0.6 percent. No other casino game provides bait quite so tempting.

Major casinos will often have as many as six or seven crap tables going full blast. At each table there can be from 20 to 30 players along with the four or five house men who supervise the game. In contrast with other games in which the equipment is handled only by employees, the players themselves roll the dice and can bet with or against the house — or the shooter — as they please. This gives them a greater sense of participation and personal control over their own fate than is to be had in any other casino game.

Prime elements in the excitement generated by a good crap game include the suspense of watching the little cubes bounce around, the players' pervasive sense of personal involvement, and the infectious enthusiasm that often develops when a sizeable group of people with a common purpose is gathered together. But the most direct contribution to excitement comes from the game itself.

After a point has been established, the shooter's task is to keep rolling the dice until he rolls either a 7 or the number that happened to be the "point." The more throws it takes him to reach a decision one way or the other, the greater the suspense all around the table, because with each new throw, large amounts of money will change hands and many of the bets on the table will be multiplying in size. I've seen times when 35 to 40 rolls were needed to reach a decision after a come-out — and 15 to more than 20 rolls between decisions are fairly commonplace. These are the times when aggressive players reap a bonanza, and more often than not, tell the world about it.

How the Game Is Played

For the benefit of those of you who may be completely unfamiliar with the game, I'll describe its essentials. Meanwhile, you should be aware that colorful descriptions of craps and the other popular casino games are often available for the asking in brochures put out by the major hotels and casinos.

Each player's turn to roll the dice comes when the shooter on his right has 7nd out. He then picks a pair of dice from five or six that are shoved in front of him by the house "stickman" and, after making a bet on either the pass or the don't-pass line, he rolls or throws the dice to the far end of the table. This first roll is called the "come-out." The 2 dice can show totals ranging from 2 to 12, and five of these numbers will produce an immediate (one-roll) decision.

On the come-out roll, 7s and 11s are called "naturals," and when they appear, all pass-line betters win and "don't" bettors lose. Two, 3, and 12 are called "craps," and when one of these numbers appears on a come-out, pass-line bettors lose and, unless the number is 12 in Las Vegas or 2 in Reno and Tahoe, the don't bettors win. When one of the last two numbers is "barred," it is considered to be the house number, the number that gives the house its slight edge of 1.4 percent on all line bets. Don't bettors and the house have a stand-off or "push" when one of these barred numbers is rolled on any come-out. The don't bettor would have a small advantage if one of these numbers were not barred.

Each shooter keeps the dice until he 7s out; that is, until he fails to "make" his previously established point. "Making" a point means throwing the come-out number a second time before throwing a 7. The "point" could be any come-out number other than the 5 "naturals" and craps. In other words, the same shooter continues to roll the dice after any one-roll decision, even if it is a crap.

The six remaining numbers, 4 5 6 8 9 10, are called "place" numbers and are often referred to simply as the "numbers." If one of them shows on a come-out, it becomes the "point" and the shooter attempts to throw that same number again before he throws a 7. If he succeeds, he has made a "pass" and he keeps the dice; otherwise, he has 7nd out, and the dice pass to the next shooter. When a point is made, the next roll is a come-out exactly the same as the shooter's original come-out — and the process is repeated.

The players have a wide choice of bets, all of which except pass and don't pass can be made at any time during play, and all of which except the odds on line and "come" bets have payouts that are biased in favor of the house. Pass, don't pass, come, and don't come are the only even-money propositions, but of course, they carry that 1.4 percent edge for the house. The "come" bets will be explained shortly.

To bet intelligently one should know the true odds on the bets in which he has, or may have an interest, and the house payouts on those bets. He should also understand the mathematical basis for those odds.

A pair of dice can total anything from 2 to 12 — just eleven possible totals, but since each die is a separate entity, there are 36 different ways to produce those 11 numbers. For example, a 3 can be made in two ways, 1, 2 or 2, 1. Seven appears more often than any other number because with 2 dice there are 6 different combinations which add up to 7, whereas its closest competitors, 6 and 8, can be made in only five different ways. Obviously there is just one way to make a 2 or a 12 or, for that matter, any other pair.

If you are going to play Craps, the data in Table 6 is important and should be memorized.

The only bets worth serious and continuing consideration are the "line" bets, the "come" bets, the "place" bets, and perhaps the "field" bets. I have not included the odds that, at the player's option, can be taken or laid on "line" and

THE CRAP TABLE

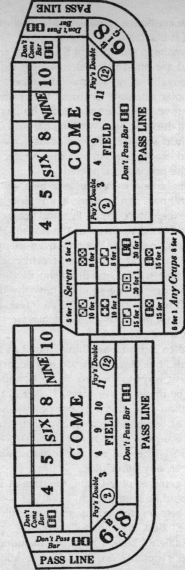

TABLE 6
True Odds and Casino Payouts at Craps

Number	Ways to make number	True odds against number on next roll	Nevada next roll payout	True odds 7 appears before number	Nevada Place bet payout
7	6	5:1	4:1	—	—
6 or 8	5	6.2:1	—	6:5	7:6
5 or 9	4	8:1	—	3:2	7:5
4 or 10	3	11:1	—	2:1	9:5
3 or 11	2	17:1	14:1*	—	—
2 or 12	1	35:1	29:1**	—	—
any crap	4	8:1	7:1	—	—

*Sometimes 15:1.
**Sometimes 30:1.

"come" bets, because those bets are really nothing more than additions to line and come bets; but their importance cannot be over-emphasized.

LINE BETS (PASS AND DON'T PASS)

When a point has been established, players are permitted to take or lay the true odds against a 7 appearing before that number is rolled again. Those odds are shown in column 5 of Table 6. Odds bets used to be limited in size to the amount of one's line bets, but nowadays many casinos allow double odds — double the amount of line bets. There is no minimum limit on the amount of odds a player may take or lay. Casinos do not pay out fractions of their minimum chips, so they usually permit odds bets to be large enough so that payouts can be made at the proper rate. Thus, when the minimum bet is one dollar, $5 odds are allowed on a $3 or $4 line bet on the 6 or 8 — or $50 odds on a $30 line bet on the same numbers. If an odd amount is bet on the 5 or 9, the house will allow an extra $1 of odds, so that it can pay out at 3 to 2. In the case of don't bettors who lay the true odds, their odds bets may be large enough so that when they win, the payout on the odds part of their bets equals the amount of their backline bet; *i.e.*, a $10 don't bet against the 4 or 10 would be entitled to lay odds of $20 to $10, or $40 to $20 whenever double odds are allowed.

MORE ON ODDS

These bets can be made, withdrawn, reinstated, or their amounts changed by the bettor at any time after a come-out. They are automatically "off" and not working on come-outs unless the bettor tells the dealer he wants them to be "working." They are the only means by which the casino's edge over the player can be reduced to as little as 0.84 percent or 0.6 percent. Double odds are what cut that advantage down to the rock-bottom figure of 0.6 percent. Many clubs allow double odds only when line bets are $5 or more.

COME AND DON'T COME BETS

These are among the most popular bets at a crap table. They are exactly the same as line bets except that they can be made at any time *after* the shooter's come-out. For the come or don't come bettor, the next roll is his come-out and he can keep on betting come or don't come every time the dice are rolled except on the shooter's own come-out. He can also take or lay odds on all his come and don't-come bets.

PLACE BETS

These, along with "line" and "come" bets, rank among the most popular of all bets at the crap table. Take another look at columns 5 and 6 in Table 6. Note that the house will offer odds that a 7 will show before any of the place numbers appear, but that the odds offered in each case are somewhat less than the true odds. Place bets are bets that any one or more than one of those numbers will be rolled before a 7 appears, and they can be made or withdrawn at any time during the play. Unless otherwise instructed by the bettor, these bets are off and not working on all come-out rolls.

The odds paid on place bets are slightly better than the combined odds available on line and come bets even when double

TABLE 7
Place Bets vs. Line and Come Bets with Double Odds

	Casino payout on:		
	6 or 8	5 or 9	4 or 10
$10 line or come bet with $20 odds	$34	$40	$50
$30 place bet	$35	$42	$54

odds are permitted. Table 7 shows the respective pay-outs on $30 wagers on the various numbers.

Place bets enjoy other advantages over come bets. When you win one, the money is yours and you can keep it, replace the bet, or add to it, as you wish. If you're betting come on each roll of the dice, as many players do, each time you win a bet it will be automatically replaced with your latest come bet — and come bets *cannot* be withdrawn at will.

On a long roll where numbers are being hit and passes made, it is relatively easy to build up your place bets to a point where a really big winning is possible. This is done by "pressing" (doubling) bets as the numbers are hit. Each time that is done, the bettor receives as change the difference between his winning and the sum it takes to double his previous bet. For example, if he had won a $10 bet on the 5 and "pressed," his bet on that number would then become $20 and he would be paid $4 as change. He had the option, of course, of taking the $14 he had won, or of raising his bet to $15 and taking back $9 in change.

During a good run, the come bettor can also recover his initial wager and insure a net profit for himself while building up his bets. He does this by drawing down only part of his winnings as they occur, while at the same time stepping up the size of his bets. However, he should always keep in mind that to win a specific come bet, his number must be hit twice between 7s, whereas only one hit is needed for any place bet to win. In my opinion, this last factor, perhaps more than any other, gives place bets a slight edge.

Of almost equal importance is the fact that a come-out 7 in the middle of hot roll can be very costly to the "come" bettor, who then loses all his outstanding come bets resting untouchable on the numbers rolling previously. His loss on that come-out would, in all likelihood, be four or five times the amount won on his line bet—even though the odds part of those earlier come bets would be returned to him. Place bets, on the other hand, are unaffected by any come-out rolls unless the player specifically instructs the dealer otherwise.

Lest I be considered biased on the question of the relative merit of place betting versus come betting, I call attention to three things which work in the come bettor's favor. Come-out 7s and 11s will occur at least twice as often as come-out craps. Since every roll is a come-out for the persistent come bettor, he stands to profit almost as much from these "naturals" as he will lose when a 7 costs him his outstanding come bets already on the table.

If the dice are "cold" and quick misses are the order of the day, the place bettor who may be on as many as 5 or 6 numbers, will take relatively severe punishment, while the come bettor is likely to have no more than one or two bets on the table when a fast 7-out occurs.

Dice seem to have a tendency to repeat numbers, so the come bettor knows that whenever he has five or six bets at risk, the chances are that there have already been two, three, or even more repeats, each of which represented profit for him. The place bettor initially assumes a 100 percent risk on the numbers he covers. If the place bettor limits his risk by placing only one or two numbers, he can be frustrated when a long roll comes along and other numbers are hit repeatedly while his chosen numbers just sit there. Of course, the same thing can happen to the conservative come bettor who has only one or two come bets out at any one time. But those come bettors who play the game aggressively, keep right on betting come and cash in on all the numbers which repeat. (Note: I have seen a 6 repeat as many as 14 times in between 7s.)

Even though I favor place bets, I'm willing to concede that the choice is close. You pays your money and takes your own choice. Whichever way you go, there is bound to be plenty of action — and that's the beauty of craps. Twenty to 25 rolls between 7s are not too uncommon, and I've seen as many as 40. When this happens, numbers are being hit right and left, and everybody's happy and prospering except the house — and perhaps that lone don't bettor over there in the corner.

THE FIELD

This is usually a grouping of all seven numbers that can be rolled with two dice except the 5 6 7 and 8. A bet on the field is a bet that one of those seven numbers will show on the next roll. A win pays even money unless the winning numbers is 2 or 12. Both those numbers pay 2 to 1 on the Strip in Las Vegas and in all the Atlantic City casinos. In downtown Vegas the 12 pays 3 to 1, while in Reno and Tahoe, you get a triple payout on either one of those numbers and a double payout on the other.

Field bets are often ridiculed as being a sort of come-on designed to attract the uninitiated. Seven numbers as opposed to only four non-field numbers are superficially inviting, even though there are 20 ways those four numbers can be made, versus only 16 ways to make the seven field numbers. Thus the true odds against the field are 5 to 4, but adjusting those odds to reflect the double and triple payouts on the two extreme numbers, they become 20 to 19, equivalent to 2.56 percent house edge, which is not too bad a deal. In fact, it is by far the best deal available on any one-roll bet. Incidentally, if no odds were paid on the 2 and 12, the house advantage would be a whopping 11.1 percent.

HARD WAYS

I have not discussed the various bets you may have noticed in the center of the crap layout because none of them fit into any betting system that I care for, and because most of them are one-roll bets carrying rather high percentages against the player. However, the "hard way" bets are not the one-roll variety and they sometimes make sense when things are going particularly well. They are bets that the 4, 6, 8, or 10 will appear as a pair before it appears in any other combination and before a 7 is rolled. The hard 6 and 8 each pay 9 to 1, and the 4 and 10 pay 7 to 1. The house advantage on the hard 6 and 8 is 9 percent; it is 11 percent on the hard 4 and 10.

"Buying" A Number and the Five Percent "Vig"

Before we get on with betting systems for craps, there is one additional type of bet I have not mentioned. Players from certain parts of the country are accustomed to "buying" numbers rather than "placing" them. When you "buy" a number, you pay the house five percent of the amount of your bet (minimum $1), and if you win you will receive the true odds on your bet. Conversely, if you bet against a specific number — as you can at any time — you may pay the house five percent of the amount you hope to win and lay the correct odds against that number. "Buying" instead of placing is advantageous only on the 4 or the 10, and then only if your bet is $20 or more. If you place the 6 or 8, the house edge is only about 1.5 percent and, next to the line bets, you're getting the best deal in the casino. When you place the 5 or 9, you are giving the house an approximately four percent advantage instead of the five percent you'd be giving if you bought, but placing the 4 and 10 gives the house a six percent advantage.

CHAPTER 9

Crap Systems

The two betting procedures used by many professionals and almost all high rollers, and recommended in much of the writing on the subject are:

1. pass, come, and maximum odds, and
2. playing the numbers (placing them)

Both these systems can produce astronomical winnings with luck and proper handling. During a long roll when a lot of passes are made along with dozens of place-number hits, aggressive players often combine the two systems — and when they do, one player can have as many as 14 separate bets on the table not counting his odds or hard ways. When a series of passes is punctuated by come-out 7s, the pass-come — odds approach is not apt to fare as well as the "numbers" approach.

Rapid escalation of bets when winning is the key to maximum profit with both these systems. As a rule of thumb, each 50 percent added to one's stake can be accompanied by a 50 percent increase in the size of his bets. Many players will go up faster than that, especially after the first couple of 50 percent gains. However, I should emphasize that continuous raising of bet levels to keep pace with winnings entails risk of sudden sizeable loss, and is not to be thought of as an essential ingredient of success at the tables.

As an example of what can be accomplished without escalation, not long ago I watched an attractive young lady being indoctrinated. From all appearances she had never played craps before. She cashed $300 and began betting $5 on pass and come, taking double odds on all her bets. After a bit she may have raised her unit bet to $10 but she never went higher than that, always taking double odds. Within an hour she had left the table with more than $1,500.

PASS, COME PLUS THE ODDS

Among "high rollers" this is unquestionably the most popular of all crap systems. However, though it often wins enormous sums for its devotees, it is probably the number one contributor to that 20 percent (minimum) profit margin that all self-respecting casinos earn on the chips in play at their crap tables.

To give you a rough idea of what the system can do at a "hot" table, one evening at Caesars Palace in Las Vegas I witnessed a roll, the like of which I have never seen before or since. A well dressed gentleman held the dice for the better part of an hour; probably about 50 minutes. I don't know how many passes he made, but I'm certain that his phenomenal run of luck cost Caesars at least $150,000, and most of that money went to players at the table who were using the pass-come-plus-the-odds system.

If I were going to use this system, here's the way I'd do it. First, I'd be careful about picking a table to play at. I'd look for one where there were quite a few bets on the numbers and where the players radiated optimism, or one which had been slow but which seemed to be picking up new players as a good roll was in progress. Then I would risk no more than 1-20th of my capital initially. That means no more than one $5 come bet along with my $5 line bet, plus full odds on both bets, assuming that my stake was $300 to $400. Then when I had won $50 or so I would not raise my bets, but I would add one or two additional come bets. Later, if I won another $30 or $40, I'd probably bet come on every throw except the shooter's own come-out, but planning to resume limiting my come bets to only 1 or 2, if my bankroll should drop back to about $300. If it reached $500 or more, I'd raise my unit bet to $10; and if it reached $650 to $700, I'd probably go to $15, continuing, of course, to take full odds plus all come bets.

With this type of play, the odds received when your numbers are hit are vitally important — so it will always be to your great advantage to use it in a casino that pays double odds.

Each of us must decide for himself when to quit. I cannot

overstress the fact that the time to quit is during or immediately after a good win. If I had started with $300 and been lucky enough to run that to near $1,000 I'm sure I would be thinking of quitting — at least for that day. This would be true for me, though it needn't be for you. The fact is that using this system, it would be as easy to convert $1,000 into $5,000 as it was to reach $1,000 after starting with $300. Nevertheless, one should be aware that while it is reasonable to anticipate at least one very long roll in any two- or three-hour session, it is often foolhardy to play for more than one such roll in a single session.

PLAYING THE NUMBERS

Most of the above generalizations apply equally to System #2, but the modus operandi is a bit different. If a friend tells you that he "plays the numbers," he uses this system or some variation of it, and there are infinite variations.

The high roller who prefers "placing" to come bets is likely to start with a $25 bet plus odds on the pass line and then say to the dealer, "150 across" or "54 across." Translated, those instructions tell the dealer in the first instance to place a $30 bet on each of the five numbers other than the shooter's point. He might hand the dealer an extra $3 and say "buy the 4 and 10." (Incidentally, most casinos will charge only $1 to buy the 4 or 10 for $25 even though the charge, or "vig," is supposed to be five percent. Many casinos do not require payment of their "vig" unless you win on a number you've "bought." If you called out "54 across," the dealer would not have to be told to place $12 each on the 6 and 8, and $10 each on the other three numbers excluding the point. Place bets on the 6 and 8 pay 7 to 6, so they are almost always made in multiples of six.

From this point on, players have their own pet procedures, but our high roller would probably plan to press most of his bets on the numbers at least once before drawing down any winnings, and he might try for two or three presses on the 6 and 8. Suppose the first number hit was a 9 on which he has $30. The payout is 7 to 5, so he's won $42. If he presses, his bet on 9 becomes $60 and he receives $12 in change. Instead of pressing the 9 only, he might have told the dealer to make the 9 and 5 $50 each. If he did that and the next roll happened to be a 5 or 9, the payout would be $70, and he might say, "same bet," meaning "pay me and leave the bet as it is"; or, of course, he might tell the dealer to add to one or another of his remaining place bets.

By this time you must have a pretty fair idea of what might happen to our man's bankroll at a hot table when a lot of numbers are being hit. His main problem will be to decide how much of his winnings to draw down at any given point. Keep in mind that all or any part of these bets can be pulled by the player whenever he pleases. Since place bets do not "work" on come-outs unless the player specifies otherwise, the ideal shooter for this system is one who somehow manages to confine his 7s to come-outs, and an ideal situation is right after a shooter has rolled two or three consecutive come-out 7s.

One assumes a fairly heavy risk if he uses this system as I've described it. If, following establishment of a point, the shooter promptly 7s out — or hits only one or two non-place numbers before sevening out, our place bettor will probably lose all six of his bets, a tidy sum. However, if his plan is to try for a big win playing the numbers in this way, his risk exposure at the start can be greatly reduced. He might, for example, use one of the more conservative systems described in this book, intending to "shoot the works" only after he had won $300 or $400 of the casino's money. Or he might start out placing only the 6 and 8, or the 5 and 9 along with a pass-line bet of the same amount as his place bets. If he does this, my recommendation would be to draw down all place bets after two or three hits and not to press more than once or twice at most.

On a number of occasions I've seen some handsome winnings develop from another modified version of the above procedure. The player bets $10 to $20 on the pass line and takes the odds when a point is established, then he places the 5, 6, and 8 or the 6, 8 and 9 (three numbers other than the point) for a total of $17. Now, regardless of what happens to his place bets, his pass line bet can more than take care of possible losses in that department; meanwhile, if he is lucky enough to have a run of three or four successive passes there's a good chance that a lot of numbers will have been hit and that he will have been able to press those place bets into sizeable figures. This approach is one of the best for an aggressive player whose bankroll is not unlimited.

"FREE" DOUBLE ODDS

When you hear or read the word "free" in connection with the odds at Craps, the usual meaning is simply that the house has no edge on the odds part of your line bets. The payout on that part of your bets is made at correct odds. However, your line bets themselves, pay only even money, so the entire payout, including the odds, has to be at less than correct odds.

Okay, you'd like to avoid dilution of those odds and also to be able to eliminate your risk exposure when you have pass and come bets on the table. Here's how that can be done, while at the same time enabling you to take advantage of full or double odds with less exposure than you normally have to accept in order to get those odds.

Bet pass and don't-pass simultaneously and in the same amounts until a point has been established. Now take double odds on your pass-line bet, but do *not* lay odds on the don't bet—or any succeeding don't bet. On each following roll bet, both come and don't come until you have at least two come bets with double odds out on the table or the shoot has sevened out. In the latter event you will have lost all your odds and you'll start over with the next shooter.

If the same shooter should make his point and then come out with a 7, you'll break even on that come-out, since any odds on working come bets will be returned to you, and your don't-come bets will offset your losing come bets. Any come-out 12 while you are betting should cost you approximately one third of the average win on each of your odds bets. With this procedure you can completely eliminate all risk at any time you choose. To do this, you stop betting and instruct the dealer to draw down all your odds bets. Then neither a 7 out nor a come-out 7 or 12 can have any effect upon your net gain or loss on that sequence.

If the table has a $5 minimum, or if $5 is the smallest bet on which double odds can be taken, you have reduced your exposure at worst from $15 to $10 per bet and at best, from $15 per bet, to zero. Obviously, to do this, you have to give up something. You no longer have the 2 to 1 advantage on come-out "naturals" (7s and 11s), and come-out 12s will prove only a minor annoyance, one chance in 36 trials.

If you use this system as I do, you will have to be quite nimble and alert. In addition to my line bets, I make two come and don't-come bets, again taking odds only on the come bets and trying to have two of them working at all times. When one of my "come" numbers is hit, if that leaves me with only one such bet on the table, I make another come and don't-come bet on the next throw of the dice. If you try this, you'll find it very helpful (maybe essential) to have a partner who will make all the don't bets, while you're making all the pass, come, and odds bets.

As you can see, this system has much in common with the conventional pass, come, plus odds system previously described, but it seems to produce more consistently favorable results. I've used it about 10 times for about two hours at a clip, and have had only three small losses with it. It has no apparent mathematical advantage over pass, come and odds, but the freedom it gives one to pull out completely when he feels that the shooter may have "had it" seems quite important. That is something that can't be done with pass and come bets alone.

There are two very different ways of using the system.

The Preferred Way: Assume that you start with $5 line and come bets, plus double odds; continue until you win $150. Then use $10 line and come bets with $20 odds until you win $250 or lose $120; then $15 with $30 odds until you win $400 or lose $200; and so on.

Whenever you lose the approximate amount shown above, you go back to the next lower level. When you've won two or more bets after any come-out, you can elect to draw down all your odds if you wish. This would leave you in a completely neutral position. If you don't pull your odds after two hits and the shooter then 7s out, you will break about even.

The Other Way: This is an up-as-you-lose method. It may be advisable to start with very small bets, possibly a 25¢ crap table. Binion's "Horse Shoe" in downtown Las Vegas is one place (there are many others) where double odds are paid on $1.25 line bets.

You move up one bet level whenever you lose two or more bets after any come out. You drop back one bet level when you've won two bets at any level up to the third; beyond that bet level you drop back two levels after winning two bets. In order to drop back you can merely reduce your odds to the desired amount, or you can draw down all your odds and wait for the next come-out.

When I have played this way, I've sometimes forgotten to reduce or pull my odds after two wins. At other times, when the shooter has 7nd out, perhaps leaving me with a net loss of one bet at that level, I'll make only one come bet after the next come-out, so that my maximum loss at that same level — and at any level except the first — can never be more than three bets. I've used the following progression, starting with both $1.25 and $2.50 line and come bets:

Line & Come Bets	1.25	2.50	5.00	7.50	10.00	12.50	15.00
Odds	2.50	5.00	10.00	15.00	20.00	25.00	30.00

I have no reservations as to the merit of this system; it is good. If you intend to try it without the help of a partner, I strongly recommend that you do so at low stakes to begin with. After that, as indicated above, you may find it a bit difficult to keep up until you've had a bit of practice. After that, with or without a partner, you can take a third, fourth, or fifth come bet if you're so inclined; then if you don't care for any number that comes up, just don't take odds on that number. When your bets are well above minimum levels, you'll be right more often than not if you pull or reduce your odds bets after two hits, but big winnings will come only when you stay with a "hot" shooter who hits a long string of numbers before sevening out.

Finally, do not be misled by the smallness of the first bets in the series I've suggested for this second method of using the system. With this procedure you'll find yourself at the fourth bet level and beyond much of the time—and your win probability will be every bit as good, if not better than it was with the procedure I labelled "preferred," but your profit potential will be much smaller.

I believe *this system effectively reduces the house edge* against the player, especially as compared with the conventional pass–come–take the odds procedure. Though I've not done the related arithmetic, I estimate that the usual house percentage should be cut by as much as 67 percent when the system is used intelligently.

THE 6–8 PROGRESSION

When I want supper money I sometimes walk up to a crap table and after the come-out, place the 6 and 8 for $6 or $12 apiece. When I have one hit I draw both bets down and proceed to the dining room. If a 7 is rolled before I get my hit, I may try again, but to wind up with a decent net profit, I then have to jump the size of my bets two and one-half or three times.

The odds are 5 to 3 in my favor on each bet I've made, but there is only a 14 percent chance that I'll lose twice in succession. Using one of the following four-stage bet series, I move up my series as I lose and if there have been six or more rolls since the last 6 or 8 appeared, I sometimes begin with the second bet in my series.

Series A	1.50	6	18	54	— Bet on each number — Total risk $159
	1.75	4	6	12	— Net profit at each point
Series B	3	12	36	102	— Bet on each number — Total risk $306
	3.50	8	12	17	— Net profit at each point
Series C	6	18	54	150	— Bet on each number — Total risk $456
	7	9	15	19	Net profit at each point

Tested against 4,000 actual casino dice decisions, the above series won 1,394 times and lost 18 times. The average was one series loss for every 77 wins. If the win-loss ratio had been 52 to 1, a player would have broken even. (Mathematically, the ratio should be about 51 to 1.) In other words, if the test results hold up, in 77 trials a user of the system should realize an average profit about equal to the amount he would clear on 25 winning bets.

Since, at 50 decisions per hour, roughly four and one-half hours of play might be required to win 77 bets, one would have a nearly-even chance of playing almost that long without ever losing his bet series. If you try the system, you may find the action too slow for your taste — but a review of the figures in the preceding paragraph may persuade you that the likely compensation could be worth a bit of tedium.

It is difficult to explain the 50 percent discrepancy between my test results and a mathematical expectancy of one loss per 51 trials. The fact that no bets are made on come-outs prevents more than a single loss whenever 7s come up consecutively — but I prefer to believe that the discrepancy is just another example of the workings of what I have called the "Law of Diminishing Probability."

In the above three bet series, average net profit per winning bet would be approximately $3, $6, and $9, respectively. This means that average hourly profits would approximate $55, $105, and $160, respectively, if there were no series losses. One thing that particularly impressed me in the extensive testing of this system was the fact that there were virtually no four- or five-hour periods when it would have been a serious loser.

It can be comforting to know that the odds are with you on each and every bet you make — and also to realize that you'll probably not have to accept the loss of a single bet series if you intend to play for only an hour or two. This 6 – 8 Progression is definitely worth serious consideration.

COUNTERACTION SYSTEMS

"Counteraction" is a sort of generic term which can be applied to a number of dice systems, several of which are anything but counterproductive. As the term suggests, these are multiple-bet systems in which risk is lessened or partially neutralized by bets which tend to offset each other. If one seeks plenty of action along with good profit potential and limited risk, this probably is the area in which he should operate.

One of my all-time favorites is a variation of the "numbers" or place-bet systems previously discussed. The difference, however, is quite radical. Instead of playing the numbers alone or with a pass-line bet, I bet don't pass and then play the numbers. Superficially, these are two opposing positions, but believe me, they can be decidedly complimentary.

I begin by betting $10 or $15 on don't pass. When a point has been established I lay $10 or $12 odds against that point and "place" the five numbers excluding the point, for $5 and $6 apiece. To do this I merely hand the dealer the required chips and say to him, "26 across" or "27 across" as the case may be. I am now insured against most of the risk represented by my place bets and I have several choices as to how those bets will be handled.

1. With five place bets the most conservative procedure would be to instruct the dealer to draw down each place bet as it is hit. In this way you'd break about even or have a profit when the shooter 7nd out, even if you'd had only one hit. If seven or eight rolls of the dice yield only two place-bet wins, you should consider pulling the rest of your place bets, as well as the odds part of your back-line bet. If you do both those things, you'll be a favorite to win about $30, and the worst that can happen is that you'll break even. When your hits come more rapidly you can play for three or four of them, but it will usually pay you to pull that one surviving unhit place bet whenever you've had four hits.

2. This second procedure can win (and lose) roughly 50 percent faster than the above, but its on-balance performance for me has been superior. In this one you leave all your place bets on until you decide that it's time to pull them all off. You play for three to eight or more hits depending on the speed with which they come. After each hit you say to the dealer,

"Same bet," and he'll pay you your winnings and leave your place bet where it was. Generally you'll try for at least five hits and give some consideration to pulling the odds part of your don't bet after you've had three or more place-bet wins. This procedure will often produce profits averaging $100 per hour for extended periods, but it is definitely not designed for a "cold" table. When handled adroitly, it wins on balance, but to show you the other side of the coin, I can recall it costing me $400 in an hour's play at the same betting level we've been discussing here. That was an unusual occasion.

3. In this third and most aggressive method of combining place bets with a negative line bet, you want your don't bet to lose. It's there only to provide initial protection. You attempt to build up your win potential by "pressing" each of your place bets (doubling them) as they are hit. Each time you press you'll receive as change the difference between the amount of your place bet and the amount of the casino payout on that bet. When this change paid to you approximates the amount you could win on the odds part of your don't bet, take those odds off. Your real objective is to build a reservoir of potential profit on those place numbers. If the shooter has a long roll, he may hit 15, 20, or more numbers in the process and if he does, you'll be coining money.

To give you an idea of the velocity of this approach, starting with $5 and $6 bets, each win after three presses would be worth roughly $60 — half that after two presses. *Caution:* unless the shooter throws one or more come-out 7s, I would tend to pull or reduce the size of my place bets after three successive passes or about 20 to 25 rolls of the dice, whichever came first. (The longest stretch I've ever seen between 7s was about 40 rolls.)

One optional play you might make at the same time you remove your backline odds bet is to place the shooter's point for the same amount as your don't bet. This will deprive you of insurance no longer really needed and at the same time put you in an improved position to cash in on your place bets if the shooter makes several successive passes. Incidentally, if he does that, your place bet on his point will pay you more than you stand to lose on your remaining don't bet, while if he 7s out you'll break even on those two bets.

The above three counteraction procedures are really gradations of the same basic system. If you start with the first conservative approach of pulling your place bets as they are hit, you can move comfortably to the second and third stages as your profits build. However, there are a couple of vitally important protective measures which must be kept in mind if you wish to achieve optimum results:

Two types of sequences can be damaging. One, of course, would be very frequent come-out 7s when your don't bet is on, and the other would be a series of fast passes which were quickly followed by the shooter sevening out. So, the following countermeasures are recommended:

1. Change tables whenever 7s seem to be appearing with abnormal frequency.
2. When you have lost your don't bet as a result of the shooter making his point, *do not replace that bet* until the same shooter has 7nd out (or) until there have been a minimum of about 15 rolls since the last 7 was thrown.
3. Whenever you lose your don't bet because a new shooter's first roll is a come-out 7, regard that as a signal for caution. You can wait out the next decision or risk two or three place bets on it after a point is established, but I suggest that you *avoid* making a new don't bet until one of the conditions in (2) above has been met.

These counteraction procedures are not foolproof; no system is. But their versatility coupled with their built-in protective features puts them right at the top of the list of tough systems for the casino to beat. They can hold their own when the dice are missing and roll up sizeable profits when the numbers are being hit. While I've discussed only three basic procedures, I'm sure you will have realized that the risk factors can be reduced beyond those I've suggested. For example, place bets can be limited to the 6 and 8 only, or to just three numbers, with a corresponding cut in the size of your backline bet.

PLACING THE 6 AND 8

When you place the 6 or 8, the house advantage is only 1.5 percent. If you've placed both those numbers, the odds are 10 to 6 that one of them will be hit before the next 7 appears. Assuming that your stake is about $200, here is one of the best and most conservative ways to play these numbers:

First bet $10 on don't pass. Then, when a point is established, place the 6 and 8 for $12 apiece. As soon as one of your place numbers is hit, pull them both. Your profit will then be $24 if the shooter 7s out and $4 if he makes his point. Of course, if he should roll one or more 7s or 11s on his come-out, you would lose your don't bet. If that happens, do not replace that bet until either he has 7nd out or rolled 12 or more other numbers since the last 7 appeared.

When the shooter makes his point or when your don't bet is lost on a come-out "natural," your place bets are not affected. You should continue to play the 6 and 8 for one hit — and when you get that hit pull both of them and you'll still wind up with a small profit. Actually, I sometimes "swap horses" after one or more come-out "naturals" or craps and bet the pass line instead of the don't. When I do that I can reduce my exposure by betting just $5 on the line and $6 each on the numbers.

This is an excellent system, but like all systems it will be unprofitable at times. If I had started with $200 and found my bankroll reduced by one-half, I'd probably cut my bets in half; expecting to resume betting $10 and $12 after I'd recouped $30 to $50 of my earlier loss.

When the shooter's point is either 6 or 8, you have three options. You can place just one number (preferred) or you can reduce your risk by placing both numbers. In the latter case, you'd lose $14 if a 7 was thrown before either number was hit, but you could win $24 if the shooter hit the other number and then 7nd out. If he made his point, you'd win $4. A third option would be to place the 5 and 9 for $5 each, along with $12 on the 6 or the 8 — or, of course, you might decide to accept the edge your don't bet gave you and make no place bet at all.

On many occasions my winnings with this simple little system have approximated $100 per hour, and often while I was winning at that rate or at the more normal rate of $1 per decision, others at the table would be playing the passline along with four or more numbers and trying for really big wins. I'd feel a bit foolish as I watched them get hit after hit on the two numbers I'd placed initially and then drawn down, and their bets doubling and tripling in amount as they were pressed, but I'm certain that my overall results have been superior. I've seen thousands of dollars of winnings dissipated so often in the course of five or six adverse rolls that I've concluded that the only ways to play for the big win are (1) to quit when it happens even if the profit is less than one's target; or (2) to cut one's bets way back and then attempt to build up to a second climax.

Perhaps I should observe here that many do not agree as to the wisdom of offsetting bets. Their premise is that you need some degree of luck to win no matter what system you use, so it makes little sense to neutralize one's luck. The other day at the Las Vegas Hilton I watched a man betting the pass line along with the 6 and 8. He started with a stack of green $25 chips, betting $25 on the line, taking full odds and then placing the two numbers for $30 each. After a few wins he doubled the amount of his bets and he did not draw down his place bets after any given number of hits, though he often pulled them on what appeared to be hunches. When, after an hour or so, I left the table, he had one rack completely filled with chips — about $2,500. There was nothing really extraordinary about this; during that hour 6s and 8s had come up with more than average frequency. Using the counteraction technique, you and I might have won only $100 or so in the same hour unless we had raised the level of our bets. Well, each of us must play the game the way that best fits our pocketbook — and temperament.

There are other practical ways of employing the counteraction principle in craps, and some of them will be described in the pages that follow. However, in my opinion none of them are superior to the four I've just outlined. If you try any of these I hope you'll observe the precautions emphasized above — and remember that place bets are not affected by come-out rolls; nor are they affected if the shooter makes his point and you lose your don't bet. When that happens your place bets remain intact and you can get quite a few hits as the same shooter continues.

One last comment: these procedures are not nearly as complicated as they may appear in print. Actually, the dealers do most of the work and are very adept at anticipating your intentions. I estimate that you'll need no more than 15 to 20 minutes at the tables before you're comfortable with any one of them and in complete command of the situation.

OTHER HEDGE-TYPE SYSTEMS

I have not tested any other hedge systems, but a few of them seem to have some merit, and/or to be worth at least passing comment.

Pass Line and Any Crap: This combination bet, of course, is nothing but insurance against a come-out crap. Any crap is a one-roll bet that pays 7 to 1, whereas the correct odds are 8 to 1. The protection this bet affords makes sense only if your pass-line bet is unusually large. Otherwise, persistent use of this type of insurance is certain to be a losing proposition.

Pass-Line and Field: I've heard good things about this strange combination, and I may experiment with it some day. The two bets are made in equal amounts, so the only come-out numbers that create an immediate loss are the 5, 6, and 8. These are good numbers, and if the shooter subsequently makes his point, you break even; or, if you've taken odds on the point, you're a net winner. If, however, the shooter misses, you'll have lost both your bets.

If the come-out is an 11, you win both bets, and if it's a 2 or 12 you are a net winner of an amount equal to either one or both of your bets, depending on whether the house pays a flat

2 to 1 on both those numbers, or 3 to 1 on one of them. If the come-out is 7 or 3 you break even, and if it's 4, 9, or 10 you're an immediate winner of your Field bet and you have a chance to win both bets.

At first glance this appears to be a system which will neither win nor lose anything of consequence, but I know one frequent crapshooter who says he has done quite well with it.

Don't Pass and Come (or) Vice Versa: One day I watched a player at the Stardust Hotel betting this way and using a three-stage Martingale in conjunction with his two opposing bets. He would bet one green chip ($25) on don't and follow that with a $25 bet on come. When he won or broke even on the two bets, he'd repeat. When he lost both bets he'd also repeat, but with doubled stakes. I saw him bet four chips each way only once, and on that occasion the shooter's second throw was a 7 so he won both his bets. After a half-hour or so he left the table, apparently a pretty good winner.

The same approach in reverse — betting pass first and then don't come — would probably prove equally effective, though it involves risk of losing both bets simultaneously whenever a 7 shows on a shooter's first throw after come-out. In any case, one of these procedures could prove a rather practical strategy for a player who wished to amuse himself while taking relatively small risk.

If I were to try this system, I believe my come bet initially would be one-half the amount of my don't bet; or with double odds, only one-third that amount. My plan would be to take full or double odds on that come bet so that I'd be a net winner if it won, regardless of the outcome of my don't bet.

Don't Pass and Place the Shooter's Point — (Definitely not recommended): There is a book presently on the market authored by a man who is a casino employee and should know better. It advocates this procedure as a virtually sure way to win — "used by some of the sharpest players in the country — and never revealed to the public until now" paraphrases his description of it.

In this system, after betting don't pass, you place the shooter's point for the same amount of your don't bet. Having done that, your position become impregnable. If the shooter misses, you break even, but if he makes his point, you make the difference between the amount of your place bet and the amount of the house payout on that bet.

The only flaw in this system is that it will lose most of the time. Out of every 36 decisions you can expect to have a net loss of five of your don't bets as a result of come-out 7s and 11s. There should be about 24 instances in which a point is established, and of these the shooter can be expected to 7-out at least 14 or 15 times, causing you to break even. That leaves just 9 or 10 winning place bets, the odds differential on which is unlikely to equal those come-out losses on your don't bets, let alone show you a profit.

THE TREADMILL
ANOTHER LOW-BUDGET SYSTEM

This is a rather amusing method by which you can have all the possible numbers except the 7 working for you. This is accomplished by placing the 5, 6, and 8 along with a smaller Field bet. The amount of each bet is fixed so that all hits except for the 2 and the 12 will yield approximately the same net profit. For example, with $7 on the Field and $10, $12, and $12 on the 5, 6, and 8, respectively, most wins will net you $7, while the 2 and 12, paying odds of 2 to 1 or 3 to 1, will be worth at least double that amount.

Now this system can be used in two very different ways. It can be (1) a sort of treadmill providing lots of action but very little movement; or (2) it can be the means by which a modest stake is built into one large enough to produce sizeable profits, given quite a bit of luck.

Let's first look at the method of play which gives the system its name. Suppose, to start, you place $2 each on the 6 and 8, and just $1 on the Field, which you'll recall is a one-roll bet. Now all the numbers are covered except the 5 and 7. If any number but one of those two appears you clear at least $1 — more if the number is 2 or 12. In any case, you may now cover the 5 with a $1 (or $2) wager making the odds 5 to 1 in your favor since you have covered all the numbers except the 7, while risking a total of either $5 or $6.

Basically, this is a time killing operation, but it keeps one interested because there's action on every roll of the dice except come-outs. If a couple of long rolls should come along, there are less pleasant things to do than pulling in a dollar on every throw of the dice. To take advantage of the odds paid on place bets and improve one's chances of winning, the Field bet might be $3, with $6 each placed initially on the 6 and 8 and $5 on the 5 after the first win. That way a win on a place bet could net $4, while a Field win would be worth $3. If you were at a table where 25¢ chips were used, the last suggested bets could be divided by four and correct odds would still be paid.

In any case, after 12 or 15 rolls with no 7s showing, this line of play will have yielded a nice little profit — and at that point it might be wise to consider pulling all bets and waiting for the inevitable 7 before resuming.

TREADMILL NUMBER 2

As I stated earlier, there is another way of using this same system, one that can produce handsome profits *when and if* it succeeds. However, I probably would not refer to it at all if I were not concerned that some of you out there would stumble upon it, think you had something great, and then lose your money trying it.

It is a logical extension of the "treadmill" idea in which, instead of taking profits as they materialize, you use them to build up the size of your Field and Place bets.

Let's say you start with $10, $12, and $12 on the 5, 6, and 8, and $7 on the Field. Each hit will be worth at least $7 net. When you've had four hits your profit is $28 or more and you then raise your wagers to $15, $18, $18, and $10. Now your risk has been increased from the initial $41 to $61, but the amount of your original funds at risk has been reduced to $33. Each win at this new level will give you an average profit of $10.50, so four more hits will enable you to again increase your wagers without adding to your basic risk. At this point you raise your Place bets to $25, $30, and $30, with $15 on the Field. Now each win will be worth an average of at least $17.50, while your own funds at risk have been further reduced to $30. With a total of eight hits so far, you have cut your initial risk from $41 to $30 and 10 more hits will net you about $145 if you don't draw down all your bets, or $245 if you do.

Runs of 18 or more throws with no sevening out come along fairly often, but I question whether they occur frequently enough to justify playing for that many consecutive hits — so keep in mind that if your bets on that last round had been pulled after only four hits, your profit would have been $140 or more.

My own negative feeling about this method of play is based on testing of recorded Las Vegas rolls, but in fairness I must tell you that I know at least three players who like the system — but they do something I have been unable to do. They pick their shooters. We know, of course, that some shooters seem to be able to consistently throw lots of numbers and make lots of passes while others do not. Therein may lie the answer; just pick the right shooter.

One staunch advocate of this system operates it a bit differently from the way I described it. Instead of playing for one long roll as I would do, he plays for only two hits after any come-out. Then he pulls his bets and waits for the next come-out or the next "good" shooter. When he has scored two hits twice — four hits in all — he increases his bets just as I did in the example above. However, he does not plan to stop at $25, $30, $30, and $15, as I suggested. When and if he gets four pairs of two hits each at that level, he again raises his bets, this time to $50, $60, and $60 with $30 on the Field.

My records indicate, however, that there is a considerably better chance of one long roll hitting 18 or more numbers, than there is of nine consecutive come-outs with no 7s showing within any of the first two following rolls. So, if you decide to try this system my advice is (1) play for one long roll; (2) try to pick your shooters; (3) escalate your bets no more than twice; and (4) when you've had 10 or more hits, begin to think seriously of pulling all your bets. Amen.

PASS LINE PLUS ODDS

Now let's look at what many consider to be the soundest, simplest, and most reliable way of playing craps to win. You make just one bet, pass, and take the odds, gradually increasing your bets as you win. If this is done intelligently — and preferably in a casino where double odds are permitted — you will be giving the house almost as tough a battle as it can face in any game of chance.

The speed or slowness with which you increase your bets as you win will reflect your aggressiveness or conservatism, but whatever your tempo, you should make certain that after two or more successive passes, any miss will still leave you with a profit almost equal to, or better than, the profit you would have had if all your bets had been the same amount as your initial bet, without any odds. Let's say your initial bet was $8. With no odds, if you had won two bets and lost the next, you would be plus $8; if you had won five bets before losing, you would be plus $32.

My own approach is apt to be on the conservative side. If my stake were $300, an initial bet of $8 would be about right — for me. That $8 would be divided between the pass line and the odds — $3 on pass and as much as $5 odds. A reminder — all or nearly all casinos, whether or not they allow double odds, allow players to raise odds to the first level beyond their line bets (of $3 or more) which will enable them to pay the correct odds on the particular point. Thus, a $3 or $4 bet on the 6 or 8 would take $5 odds — or a $30 bet could take $50 odds. A $3 bet on the 5 or 9 could take either $2 or $4 odds so that the house could pay off at 3 to 2. But since the true odds against 4 or 10 are 2 to 1, the odds taken on those numbers would have to be the same or less than one's line bet.*

With single odds and a $300 stake, I would plan to escalate my line bets about as follows:

3 5 5   7 10 10   15 20 20

With double odds, my scale might be:

3 5 5   5 10 10   10 15 15

With each of those bets, except possibly my second bet in the double-odds scale, I would take the maximum allowable

---

*Except when double or triple odds are permitted.

odds. On that bet, if I were behind at the time, I might limit my odds to the amount of my line bet so that in case of a loss I would almost break even on the first two bets. My plan would be to move up the series each time the shooter made a point on which I had an odds bet. When he rolled a natural (7 or 11) or a craps (2, 3 or 12) I would stay at the same spot in my series, but if he threw two successive naturals I would advance one number. If he threw two successive craps, that would end the series for me and I'd start a new one.

With each 50 percent improvement in my bankroll, I would raise the level of all my bets by about the same percentage. Also, after winning the first five bets in a series, I might consider drawing down my winnings and placing the 6 and 8 for a total of about the amount that I'd won on the last bet in that series. Let's take a series of 27 fairly typical dice decisions to see how this procedure might work out in actual play. We'll tabulate results with both single and double odds but with the second bet in both series at single odds (Table 8).

In the hypothetical series there are 14 passes and 13 misses. Naturally I stopped at a favorable point, as you should when you play. Although the progressions I've used are quite conservative, I feel, in the long run, that they will do as well or better than much steeper series — and with considerably less wear and tear on the bettor's nervous system.

If you intend to use this system, it will be advantageous to select a casino where at least three tables are active. This will make it easy to change tables when the one you've been using seems to be cooling off. While hot and cold streaks in craps are often short-lived, they sometimes last for an hour or more — so table selection can be quite important.

If you like this basic approach but prefer not to be so dependent on sequences of consecutive passes, you can be a "switch hitter," betting both pass and don't and using a series of escalating bets like those previously discussed in connection with what I've called the "Straight-Up" system. When I do this I tend to favor the "Pattern" method of bet selection; and when it calls for a pass-line bet of, say, $20, I may bet $10 on the line expecting to take from $5 to $10 odds, depending upon which number becomes the point. Then, if a natural (7 or 11) is

TABLE 8
Comparative Results, Double vs. Single Odds (Passline Bets)

Line bet	Come-out no.	Odds: Single	Double	Win (+) Lose (−)	Result ($): Single odds	Double odds
3	6	5	5	−	(8)	(8)
3	10	3	6	−	(6)	(9)
3	9	4	6	+	9	12
5	2	−	−	−	(5)	(5)
5	6	5	5	−	(10)	(10)
3	8	5	5	−	(8)	(8)
3	10	3	6	+	9	15
5	5	6	6	+	14	14
5	5	6	10	−	(11)	(15)
3	12	−	−	−	(3)	(3)
3	5	4	6	+	9	12
5	6	5	5	+	11	11
5	9	6	10	+	14	20
5	4	5	10	−	(10)	(15)
3	4	3	6	+	9	15
5	8	5	5	−	(10)	(10)
3	7	−	−	+	3	3
3	6	5	5	−	(8)	(8)
3	8	5	5	−	(8)	(8)
3	4	3	6	−	(6)	(9)
3	2	−	−	−	(3)	(3)
3	5	4	6	+	9	12
5	4	5	5	+	15	15
5	6	5	10	+	11	17
5	9	6	10	+	14	20
10	7	−	−	+	10	10
10	9	10	20	+	25	40
				Net + 66		+ 105

thrown on the come-out, I'm ahead of the game and I may make the same bet or one slightly smaller on the next roll. Playing this way, naturals and come-out craps are treated exactly as if you were betting the pass line only. Following two naturals you move up one notch; and after two craps you start a new series unless you happen to be betting don't pass when they occur.

Before we leave this very basic and sound approach I want to make it clear that bets can be escalated a good deal more rapidly than the examples shown above and still fall within the parameters of reason. Here, for example, is a series where after the first win you would draw down $5, after the second win another $5, after the third win $10, after the fourth win $20, and after the fifth win $30:

    10   15   25   40   60   90

After five winning bets at even money, you've won $150, having risked only $10, and you're in a position to risk $90 on your next bet knowing that if you lose you'll still be $60 to the good. Note that if you'd won five bets at $10 each and lost your sixth bet of $10, your net gain would be only $40.

Now let's see how you might have fared if you'd been using double odds and the shooter had made five consecutive passes without any naturals. We'll break down each number in the above series into two numbers, one for our line bet and the other for odds; viz:

| Pass-Line | 5 | 5 | 10 | 15 | 20 | 30 |
| Odds | 5 | 10 | 15 | 25 | 40 | 60 |

If the shooter now makes the 5, 6, 10, 8, and 9, in that order, your odds on the first bet would have been $6 instead of $5 so that you could be paid at 3 to 2, and the payouts on each of these bets would have been $14, $17, $40, $45, and $80, respectively, for a total of $196. So, if you continued this series but lost your next bet of $90, you'd still retain a profit of $106 on your starting investment of $11. As for me, after those five wins, I'd probably pull back to a $10 line bet with $20 odds. I would give no thought to placing the 6 and 8 because there hadn't been a single 7 during the run. If, on the other hand, the shooter's next two come-out rolls were 7s, I'd be only too happy to bet the $90 and maybe throw in two or three small place bets for good measure.

NEW SHOOTER SYSTEM
(Bet with Him)

There is a semi-valid reason for the widespread superstition or suspicion that it is unwise to bet against a new shooter on his first come-out. The previous shooter had just sevened out, so a wager that the next shooter will not miss, in effect is an even-money bet that there won't be two successive misses. Of course, a don't bet against a new shooter really is an even-money proposition, but I know one old-time gambler who insists that the simplest and surest way to win he knows is to bet pass on each new shooter, using a three-stage Martingale progression such as 10-20-40.

When this man loses his first bet, he simply doubles up, and if he loses his third bet in the series, he starts over — just one bet on each new shooter. He says that since it's a rather boring procedure, he rarely uses it, but that it has seldom, if ever, failed him.

I have never tried the system, but it tests out nicely on paper. You see, when you use this procedure you are really betting 7 to 1 that there won't be four misses in succession. (The previous shooter having 7nd out, you'd have four misses if the next three shooters also missed.) Thus, betting this way, you can imagine that you're in the comfortable situation of a man offering 7 to 1 odds on a 15 to 1 proposition. Of course, if that were actually the case, you'd have found the "millenium." I agree, however, that the probabilities definitely favor you — you shouldn't expect to lose those three consecutive bets once in every eight tries.

I have tested this system without using odds against 3,480 crap decisions in Las Vegas, and the results were extremely good; in fact, so good that I plan to give it the acid test the next time I find myself in Nevada. Those 3,480 decisions represented about 64 hours of playing time. In that period, with a 10-20-40 betting scale, this system would have won $1,560, equivalent to roughly $24 per hour. So, if you like money enough to accept a little boredom in return for it, it should prove to be well worth the effort.

CHAPTER 10

The Don't Bettor
(The Man Nobody Loves)

In every gathering of dice devotees there are always a few hardy and persistent nonbelievers, sometimes called "wrong" bettors. At the tables you will occasionally notice an old-timer — or a not-so-old-timer betting nothing but the backline or don't-come or both. You'll see him but you won't hear him, since he tends to dislike attention. More often than not his bets are larger than the average, but when it comes his turn to throw the dice, chances are he'll forego that pleasure, not because he doubts the probable outcome, but he doesn't relish the resentment he will generate among many of his fellow players if the dice do what he wants them to do; nor does he enjoy the scornful tone with which the stickman will loudly announce, "He's shooting from the don't."

Due to the fabled perversity of dice, the pass-line bettor's level of confidence is apt to rise noticeably whenever a don't bettor attempts to make the dice do his bidding, but there will be some among those "right" bettors who will actually resent the fact that the fellow had the temerity to handle the dice at all. After all, his object was to cause everyone else at the table to lose, was it not? His status is much like that of a boardroom short seller during a roaring bull stock market. He may be tolerated, but he'll surely be unloved. In this connection it is well to keep in mind that in craps no bet is against the shooter or "with the house." All line bets are simply with or against the dice.

Although the don't bettor would have a slight edge in a back room or alley game of craps, he has no perceptible advantage in a casino which usurps the 12 or the 2 as its own private property and makes those numbers fine examples of its altruism — Heads they win; tails you break even. On the contrary, he has certain disadvantages. On come-outs the odds against him are 8 to 3 since 7s and 11s appear that much more often than 2s and 3s (or 3s and 12s). When the dice are "cold" he'll win, but even if he's playing very aggressively and betting don't come along with the backline, his winnings cannot accumulate at anything like the speed at which they might if he'd been wagering the same amounts on the pass line while the dice were "hot."

The primary disadvantage of the don't bettor lies in the fact that there is no way on earth for him to take advantage of the odds available to the pass-line bettor. Thus, to win any given sum, he must risk a good deal more money than the player who bets with the dice. When he's on the backline or don't-come and wants to make a maximum bet against the point, he must "lay" the correct odds (pay them) rather than receive them, as he would if he were betting with the dice. Moreover, if he wishes to bet against a specific number, in addition to laying the true odds against that number, he must pay the house a five percent premium or "vig" for the privilege. By way of contrast, you will recall that none of the place bets except the 4 and 10 carry that high a premium for the house or liability for the player.

You may wonder why I take the trouble to recite all the negative aspects of betting against the dice. There are two reasons: First, many neophytes assume wrongly that since most players bet with the dice and lose, the obvious and easy way to win must be to bet the other way. Second, there are many persons whose temperaments are such that they're more comfortable betting don't than they would be otherwise. For them there are procedures and techniques which tend to offset the disadvantages previously mentioned and to maximize profit potential. Let's face it, there are many times when the nays have it and the ayes have nothing but grief. So I'll tell you what I consider to be sound procedure if you are a don't bettor or expect to be one.

TABLE 9
Don't Bettors' Advantage After Point Is Established

Point	No odds	Full odds	Double odds
4 or 10	33.3 percent	14.2 percent	9.1 percent
5 or 9	20 percent	9.1 percent	5.9 percent
6 or 8	9.1 percent	4.3 percent	2.8 percent

First and foremost, if you habitually bet don't, cultivate the habit of seldom — repeat — seldom — laying odds on your don't-pass bets. I cannot tell you why so much misinformation on this subject has been circulated by self-proclaimed authorities and professionals and how it has managed to slip by the censors, but it has. They tell you that by laying full odds, you cut the house percentage to 0.84 percent and that laying double odds cuts it still further to about 0.6 percent.

Now let's look at the arithmetic. The point is 4 or 10 and you have a $10 don't bet. There are six different ways that two dice can come up totaling 7, but only three ways they can total either 4 or 10. The odds, therefore, are 2 to 1 in your favor, which means that in three trials you are expected to win twice, lose once and wind up with a profit of $10. Now suppose you lay full odds of 20 to 10, which would make your total bet $30 to $20. With that bet if you win twice and lose once you will win $40 and lose $30, so your net gain will be $10, just as it was before you laid the odds. You'd have the same end result if you'd laid double odds, making your total bet $50 to $30. In either case, by laying odds you'd win a *little* more if your success ratio exceeded the 2 to 1 norm, but you'd lose a *lot* more if that ratio proved to be less than 2 to 1.

The above logic applies equally to the other four place numbers. A highly regarded research organization which has no connection with the gambling fraternity describes the don't bettor's advantage after a point has been established as "overwhelming." I suggest you re-examine Table 9, above.

You look at the figures and say to yourself, "Well, the bettor still has an edge over the house after he's laid those odds, so why shouldn't it be to his advantage to increase the size of his bets? Won't he be sure to win more in the long run if his bets are larger?" The answer, my friends, is that it would be to his advantage only *if his increased wagers were made at less than the correct odds.*

In case the above logic is not entirely clear to you, let's assume that two men are betting on a 2 to 1 proposition and their results run exactly true to form. One of these men makes 1,000 bets of $1 at even money, while the other makes 1,000 bets of $10 each, laying 2 to 1 odds. Which man will win more? I trust the answer is obvious. The first man will win $333, while the second man will break exactly even.

Presumably our backline bettor has lost eight of his bets on come-outs for every three such bets that he's won. Now that the shooter is trying to make a point, there is no longer a house percentage; there is a player percentage. That being so, chances are that the very next decision will be in his, the bettor's, favor. That reasoning would seem to partially justify an odds bet no matter how much dilution of the player's advantage it entailed — but as I've tried to make clear, that reasoning will not hold up if it is applied consistently.

I personally bet the backline quite often, but my don't bets simply reflect my feeling at the moment or the bet selection system I happen to be using. I never bet don't continuously and exclusively — and since I'm always using a progression of one sort or another or a system calling for switching from pass to don't, I almost never lay odds on my backline bets.

However, for the benefit of you who may now be, or may become persistent don't bettors, I have carefully analyzed my own records and studied the procedures of players who appeared to enjoy some success betting that way. Here are my conclusions in the form of general and specific advice:

1. Never lay double odds. In general, tend to avoid laying any odds when you are behind. The 6 and 8 are the best points against which to lay odds, but if you're tempted, perhaps you should count to 10 before taking action.

2. Never make more than two don't-come bets — or three at most.

3. Tend to skip the first come-out of any new shooter — and his next come-out also if his first one is a 7, 11, or crap.

4. Seldom take more than two successive losses — three at most — from one shooter in a single series of passes. Stop betting.

5. Look for spots where there have been an abnormal number of throws — 15 or so — with no 7s, and jump in. The water's likely to be fine.

6. Take your play to tables which are relatively quiet and uncrowded; not many bets on the numbers and the atmosphere subdued; or conversely, to a table which has been "hot" for more than an hour and seems to be in the process of cooling off.

7. Vary the amount of your bets using one of the progressions or money-management systems described earlier in this book.

8. This one may be controversial, but my records show that it is quite likely to prove a money maker or money saver. *Don't bet the backline at all;* instead bet don't come on the first throw, or the first two throws only after a point has been established. In this way you will miss those sequences of 7s and 11s that occur so often on come-outs.

For players who bet only sporadically and like to pick their spots, the best time to step in with a don't-pass or don't-come bet is right after a shooter has thrown 10, 20, or more numbers before sevening out, or after a new shooter has thrown his first pass. If a shooter has made several successive passes with no come-out 7s before his last roll, that "spot" would be just about ideal.

If one makes a sizable don't bet and wishes to protect himself against an immediate come-out 7, he can make a one-roll bet against the 4 or the 10 at the same time. He would have to lay 2 to 1 odds on that "insurance" bet and some casinos might also charge him their five percent "vig," but there would be no "vig" if he pulled his insurance bet before he'd either won or lost it. On a single roll the true odds against either the 4 or 10 are 11 to 1. (A few clubs, notably the Horseshoe in downtown Vegas, do not charge any "vig" on bets against the 4 or 10 if and when those bets lose. Most casinos, however, do collect their 5 percent "vigs" on all lay bets, win or lose.)

BETTING AGAINST THREE CONSECUTIVE PASSES

The odds against a player making three passes in a row are 7 to 1. However, my records of 3,625 crap decisions (not hand-picked) indicate that the likelihood of any shooter making three passes is somewhat less than once in eight trials. In one Las Vegas session of 235 decisions there were 123 misses as opposed to 112 passes. In that session a player who bet $10 on don't pass *whenever there was a new shooter*, and when he lost, continued with a maximum of two more bets of $20 and $40 *against the same shooter*, would have won $490. In roughly four hours he would have won a net of $10 one hundred and five times and lost his $70 bet series only eight times. This, of course, was an exceptional case.

The same procedure applied to 3,625 decisions yielded a net profit of $2,040, equivalent to roughly $30 per hour of play. There were two 10-hour sessions that produced losses of $340 and $200, respectively, and in the course of play the biggest loss sustained at any time was about $400. These figures take no account of come-out 12s, or the exercise of judgment by the bettor. There is no way to evaluate the relative importance of these two factors, but my guess is that they just about offset each other.

If you try this system or some variation of it, your don't bets should usually be limited to three against the same shooter. If you lose three bets, stop and wait for the next shooter. However, in those rare instances when a shooter makes six successive passes, the odds will be with you if you jump in after the sixth pass and start a new three-bet series.

Many don't bettors are superstitious about lady shooters and also about any new shooter's initial come-out. They often skip those bets. If you wanted to play cautiously, you might do the same thing. You'd have slower action, but if the decision you skipped happened to be a pass, you would then be giving only 7 to 1 odds on what many would consider an almost 15 to 1 proposition. You'd be betting that the shooter wouldn't make four consecutive passes (three after his first pass). Another conservative ploy would be to skip the next decision whenever there is a come-out "natural" or crap.

I have suggested using a three-stage Martingale, but this system will work just as well, with less risk and smaller profit if one's bet series is 5 5 10 or 10 10 25 or 10 10 30 or 2 2 6. If you used this type of series, you'd start a new series whenever you won a bet, but if you won the second bet in your series after losing the first, you would do no better than break even. The third bet in your series would be made only when you had lost two successive bets against the same shooter.

DON'T BETS AND THE "STEP LADDER"

Although I've recommended a system in which you double your don't bets twice after losses, I prefer the opposite approach as a general thing.

The "Step Ladder" type of progression can perform nicely for a confirmed don't bettor. On one occasion recently, using a variation of that system, raising and lowering my bets in $10 and $5 increments, I made $600 in about two and one-half hours. Most of my bets were on the backline (don't pass), and my biggest bet was either $35 or $40. Here is the basic betting sequence I used for winning bets:

    5   10   15   25   35

When I lost any bet, I dropped back $5. If I reached the $15 level, whether that bet was won or lost, I moved up $10 after each winning bet until I started a new bet series. The following series of passes (P) and misses (M), will illustrate:

M	M	M	P	P	M	P	P	M	P	P	
−5	−5	−5	5	10	(15)	10	20	−30	25	35	(Net, $45)

When I won the first three bets in a series, I usually terminated that series and started a new one.

A (seemingly) safer way of doing the same thing would be to escalate more slowly at the beginning of a series, as, for example:

TABLE 10
Escalating and De-escalating Winning and Losing Bets

	Win/Lose:									Net result
	+	−	+	−	−	+	+	−	+	
Bettor A	20	(30)	20	(30)	(20)	10	20	(30)	20	(20)
Bettor B	20	(30)	25	(35)	(30)	25	35	(45)	40	+5
Bettor C	20	(35)	30	(45)	(40)	35	50	(65)	60	+10

    5   6   8   10   13   16   20   25

moving up with the above spacing as you win and dropping
back just $1 after each loss. I've done this a number of times
with fairly good results, but somehow the results have never
approached my scores with the faster progression shown on
the preceding page.

A final word of caution: As you win and lose, do not make
the mistake of moving up and down a bet series at the same
rate. That is the flaw in the Ascot system. The whipsaws tend
to eat up your profits. To illustrate, observe the sequence of
wins and losses in Table 10.

Even though there are five plusses against four minuses in
the Table 10 sequence, the first bettor who moved up 10 when
he won and down 10 when he lost, wound up losing 20. The
other two bettors escalated winning bets twice and three times
respectively, as rapidly as they lowered their losing bets —
and both had small profits for the same sequence.

You may have noted that if one more plus had been added
to the sequence, the variance in the three results would have
been much more dramatic. Reading from top to bottom, the
respective scores would then have been plus 10, plus 55, and
plus 85. If one more minus had been added, the disparity
between results would have been relatively minor.

CHAPTER 11

Roulette

As played in this hemisphere, with two zeros on most of the wheels, roulette is not, as a rule, an ideal game for gamblers who want their casino visits to be profitable. It is always, however, an excellent vehicle for fun and relaxation. At almost all roulette layouts one can play for very small stakes and while away the time without serious financial risk.

With the typical American wheel the house percentage is usually said to be 5.26 percent on all bets but one, or more than eight times the lowest percentage bets available in craps. Furthermore, the true odds against any of the so-called even bets in roulette are 20 to 18 or 10 to 9, which looks more like an 11 percent edge for the house. Despite those rather forbidding odds, there are thousands of inveterate roulette players, of whom a very small minority manage to win on balance. Oswald Jacoby, the famous bridge player and games analyst, has estimated that an average player making 500 bets has no better than a 10 percent chance of finishing with a profit.

The prime requisites for winning at roulette are (1) a sound money-management system; (2) concentration, plus a system for keeping track of the numbers that come up; (3) self-discipline; and (4) at least average luck. All of the systems described in chapters 5, 6, and 7, as well as the bet-selection procedures in chapter 2, can be applied to any of the 6 even-money bets in roulette.

The game itself is extremely uncomplicated, and despite the odds against consistent winning, there are good reasons for every casino patron to familiarize himself with it. When one is under pressure, the best antidote is to remove himself at least temporarily from the source of the pressure. Roulette tables in our country are apt to be uncrowded and the tempo of play unhurried. The atmosphere is likely to be pleasant, and, as I've already indicated, one can play for hours if he wishes to, without serious financial risk. In Nevada, betting minimums are usually $1 for a bet on any one of the outside propositions, the dozens, columns, and even-money bets, and $1 in the center on the numbers. The dollar bet in the center may be divided into as many as 10 different bets if 10¢ chips are used, or four bets if the lowest denomination chip is 25¢.

Incidentally, roulette is an excellent party game. Nice little sets for home use with convenient betting layouts can be purchased for around $25. When played with friends the usual method of evening things up is to take turns as banker. Another popular device is to ignore the double zero and not count any spin when the little ball lands in that slot. In any case, a home set can be fun and is a great way to completely familiarize oneself with the game.

A home set will also help prepare you for your travels abroad if you plan to visit some of the famous clubs and casinos in London and on the continent where roulette is by far the most popular of all the games. The rules abroad are ever so much more favorable for the player than they are here. Wheels have only a single zero, and if you have a bet on one of the even chances, when the zero comes up you lose only half that bet, or your bet may "go to prison," as they so quaintly put it. In the latter case your bet stays on the table and if you win the next spin, the money you bet is yours; otherwise it goes to the house. In either case, the house percentage on such bets is cut down to a paltry 1.35 percent which is one-fourth the advantage enjoyed by most casinos on this side of the Atlantic, and even less than the casino edge on line bets in craps.

The typical physical set-up in this country consists of a large saucer-shaped perfectly balanced wheel at one end of a table which accommodates no more than five or six seated players. The betting layout covers much of the table area and the dealer or croupier stands behind the table and spins the wheel after he has collected the losing bets and paid the winners on the previous spin. He spins the wheel slowly as a rule, and then he spins a small ivory, plastic, or metal ball along the outer rim of the wheel in the direction opposite from that of the wheel itself. In due course gravity pulls the little ball down to the center part of the wheel where there are 38 evenly spaced slots,

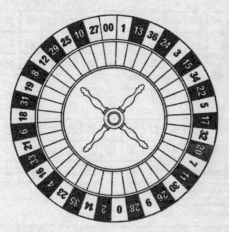

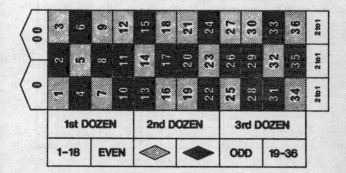

ROULETTE BETTING LAYOUT

2-number Combinations

3-number Combinations

4-number Combinations

5-number Combination

6-number Combinations

EXAMPLES OF COMBINATION BETS

into one of which the ball will slide and come to rest. Each slot is numbered and colored to correspond with the numbers and colors on the betting layout. The numbers from 1 to 36 are half red and half black; the zero and double-zero are green. The dealer calls out the winning number and usually places a marker over that number on the betting layout for the benefit of players who might have difficulty seeing the bottom part of the wheel where the little ball had stopped.

The solid numbers in the diagram on page 137 are black, and the shaded numbers, except for the 0 and 00, are red. The zeros are usually green. A single chip placed in the numbered area can be a bet on one number or on groupings of from two to six numbers. Those bets are made as indicated in the diagrams on page 138.

The house payout on various combinations of numbers is:

1 number ....35 to 1
2 numbers ....17 to 1
3 numbers ....11 to 1
4 numbers ....8 to 1
5 numbers ....6 to 1*
6 numbers ....5 to 1

The outside bets on the roulette layout are the ones we're most concerned with. They consist of the three columns of 12 numbers each, the three dozens as shown in the diagram and the six even-money bets at the bottom of the diagram, each of which covers 18 numbers. The dozens and the columns pay 2 to 1.

Most of the systems described in Chapters 6 and 7 can be used on the even bets, red, black, high, low, odd, and even. The previously recommended bet-selection methods also seem to apply as well to roulette as they do to craps, with the edge going to the "pattern" procedure.

The almost infinite variety of combination bets that one can make in roulette contribute to the game's fascination. But no

*This is the only bet in roulette on which the house percentage is slightly higher than 5.26 percent.

matter how one bets, or how many numbers or groups of numbers he covers, the percentage against him remains constant. That is, it remains constant with a single exception. There is just one way that a five-number combination can be covered with a single chip (see diagram, page 138). One chip properly placed will cover the 1, 2, 3, 0, and 00. If a $5 wager on that combination wins, the payout is 6 to 1, or $30, but if $1 had been placed on each of those numbers, the payout would have been $31 ($35 less the $4 bet on the losing numbers).

An amusing and often confusing feature of the betting layout is to be found in the columns which pay 2 to 1. Each column has 12 numbers, half of which are odd, half even, half low (1 to 18), and half high (19 to 36) — but for some obscure reason in columns 2 and 3, red and black numbers are divided unevenly. Column 3 has eight reds and four blacks, while column 2 has eight blacks and four reds. This anomaly often persuades players that by betting one of the colors along with the column in which the other color predominates they will somehow give themselves a real advantage. They overlook the fact that this strategy — sometimes called the "Cuban" — tends to deprive them of a full payout when their bet on the color wins, for the odds then are more than 3½ to 1 that they will have lost their column bet. My own judgment is that if one feels that one or the other color is due to come up, his interests will be best served if he bets the column in which that same color predominates. Ignoring the two zeros, betting that way would give him an even chance of winning his color bet, plus an almost even (44.4 percent) chance of also winning the column bet which would pay him 2 to 1 odds.

Most roulette players seem to favor the "dominance" theory of bet selection. That is, they tend to bet that the wheel will continue to do what it has been doing; that the numbers that have been coming up will continue to come up. Whether this is due mainly to suspicion of wheel imperfections or that the croupier somehow is able to control his spins, I cannot say. But one can understand the reactions of players who see a lot of repeats and observe that the wheel and the little ball always seem to be spun at exactly the same speed, and with the same timing.

Many authorities believe that with practice, the croupier can and does acquire a measure of control as to the segment of the wheel where the ball will drop, but this is disputed by others. It is generally agreed, however, that cheating by the use of magnetic devices was a common practice in certain areas, notably Havana in the pre-Castro days. As for imperfect or off-balance wheels, there have been many stories of fortunes made by sharp individuals whose modus operandi was to find one of these and then milk it until the casino finally discovered what was wrong. Most of these stories are probably fictitious since it is obvious that an imperfect wheel would constitute a clear and present danger for the house rather than for the player. The wheels used in most resorts are made to extremely close tolerances and they are usually checked every 24 hours. Not only that, but in those casinos that have several wheels, the usual practice is to change their positions in the early morning hours to foil any patron who might intend to latch on to a particular wheel he'd found the day before and which appeared to be biased.

The tempo of a roulette game at which there are five or six players does not seem especially hurried, but when there are three or less at the table, it is definitely fast. It is as if the house wanted to make sure that the players had insufficient time to plan any reasoned betting strategy. In this country the average spin rate is said to be 80 to 90 spins per hour, whereas in England and France the average hourly rate is only 25 to 30 spins.

The difference in the tempo here and abroad reflects three things: (1) There are fewer players at a typical American table, hence less work for the dealer after each spin; (2) The practice here is to start a new spin almost as soon as settlements for the previous spin have been completed, without waiting for players to finish placing their bets (players are allowed to continue placing bets while the little ball is spinning around); (3) Payment of winning bets is easier and faster here than in many European casinos, since each American player is given chips of a color used by no other player at his table. These chips can represent any denomination that the player chooses. In French roulette, the color of a chip indicates only its redemption value; players do not have their own individual colors, so disputes often arise as to who placed this or that winning bet.

CHAPTER 12

Roulette Systems

The typical roulette player uses no real system. He is entranced by the idea of those 35 to 1 odds paid on the individual numbers and he is almost sure to have certain pet numbers that he'll bet fairly persistently. As a rule, he'll scatter his 10¢, 25¢, or 50¢ chips all over the center part of the layout, concentrating them at one or two spots — while dreaming of the possibility of a double hit on a number which could pay him 1,225 to 1.

Our system player's approach is quite different. Whether he's going to play for "peanuts" or real money, he should have pen and paper and chips of at least two differing denominations, perhaps 25¢ and $1, or $1 and $5. If he intends to use one of the previously described money-management systems (progressions), he may not need the pen and paper, but they could help him spot an occasional promising side bet, regardless of what system he happens to be using. The different colored chips will aid him with his bet selection (see Chapter 2).

However, if our system player plans to confine most of his bets to "sleepers" (numbers, colors, columns, dozens, etc. that haven't come up for abnormally long periods), then a small notebook will enable him to keep track of the various things which he'll want to follow. The best way I know to have a ready record of everything that has happened and hasn't happened at your table is to use your notebook as indicated in the diagram on page 144.

If your notebook is lined horizontally, that will help you see at a glance the order of occurrence of all prior spins. In the diagram on page 144 you will note, for example, that three of the first four spins were red and were also in column 3. You see also that the last four spins have been odd numbers. If you

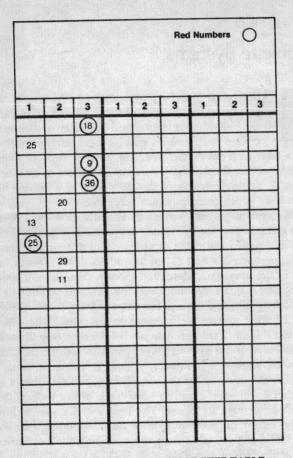

			Red Numbers ◯					
1	**2**	**3**	**1**	**2**	**3**	**1**	**2**	**3**
		(18)						
25								
		(9)						
		(36)						
	20							
13								
(25)								
	29							
	11							

RECORD KEEPING AT A ROULETTE TABLE

have six sets of the three columns on facing pages, you can be looking at the last 50 to 100 spins much of the time, and it should be quite easy to spot "sleeping" finals, as well as a variety of other abnormalities.

In this connection I want to stress something that every person who gambles should commit to memory and take to heart. The law of averages always works in the long run, but beyond a reasonable point, it should never be relied upon to work in the short run. Earlier I may have referred to "the immediate improbability of the probable." Believe me, that catch phrase is one to ponder, no matter what your project of the moment happens to be. In this case its application simply means that when you decide to bet against the continuance of some abnormal sequence of events, you should also decide how many times and how much money it might be reasonable to bet that the sequence would end — and, *having made your decision, never, never deviate from it.* (I've seen the same color come up 15 times in succession, and the same 2 to 1 column come up nine times in a row.)

"Sleepers"

In Table 11 we have assumed the use of some type of Martingale such as 2-4-8, or a modified Martingale for betting on "sleepers." The fourth column reflects that assumption. If you don't believe in the "law of diminishing probability" as I do, my theory that sleepers offer better-than-average betting situations will not impress you, and you may then wish to ignore the third column. In either case, the indicated number of bets with a Martingale-type progression makes sense. I'll show you later how to make 15 such bets on a "final" or any three- or four-number combination, without getting up into the stratosphere.

Occasionally you'll have four or five repeats of the same column or dozen — the most I've ever seen was nine — and you may be tempted to bet both of the "sleepers." If you do that, you'll be risking $2 to net $1 of profit and with two sizeable bets it might be well to consider a bit of insurance on the

TABLE 11
"Sleepers" — When and How Often to Bet on Them

Bet	House payout	Bet only after how many "no-shows"	Maximum number of bets on one sleeper
Red/Black	even money	3 to 4	3
High/Low	even money	3 to 4	3
Odd/Even	even money	3 to 4	3
Columns	2:1	4 to 5	5 to 6
Dozens	2:1	4 to 5	5 to 6
4-number finals	8:1	20 to 30	15
3-number finals	11:1	25 to 40	15

house numbers. A two-way bet on zero and double zero pays 17 to 1. My own preference in that situation is to pick the column or dozen that has slept the longest and bet on it alone. Meeting the situation that way, if my timing has been good, I'm going to be paid 2 to 1 odds on a bet that I feel is almost as promising as some even-money wagers.

SLEEPING FINALS

Now let's consider those three and four number combinations that pay 11 to 1 and 8 to 1, respectively. In that category, sleeping "finals" are relatively easy to spot if you keep the kind of running record that I've recommended. "Finals," you'll recall, are the groupings of numbers with the same last digit. Finals ending with zero through 6 have four numbers each, while those from 7 through 9 have three numbers each. Here is a novel way to bet them.

We'll use 25¢ chips and on the first round we're going to make five bets of one chip each on our four numbers (or three numbers, as the case may be). On the second round, make four bets of two chips each; next round, three bets of three chips on each number; then two bets of four chips on each number; and finally, one bet of five chips on each number. Of course, we would have stopped and perhaps tried another sleeping final if we had won any of those bets. In the case of the four-number

TABLE 12
System for "Sleeping Finals"

Total bet ($)	Units on each bet	Net profit ($): Bet number:	1	2	3	4	5
Finals 0 to 6							
5.00	1		8.00	7.00	6.00	5.00	4.00
8.00	2		11.00	9.00	7.00	5.00	
9.00	3		11.00	8.00	5.00		
8.00	4		10.00	6.00			
5.00	5		10.00				
35.00 Risk							

Total bet ($)	Units on each bet	Net profit ($): Bet number:	1	2	3	4	5
Finals 7 to 9							
3.75	1		8.25	7.50	6.75	6.00	5.25
6.00	2		12.75	11.75	9.75	8.25	
6.75	3		15.00	12.75	10.50		
6.00	4		16.50	13.50			
3.75	5		18.75				
26.25 Risk							

finals we risked a total of $35, and our risk on a three-number final would have totaled $26.25.

Our anticipated net winnings at any point in these series are shown in Table 12.

The important thing to remember about progressions on sleepers is never to continue betting on one that has just cost you your entire bet series. Look for another candidate for your attention. However, it is a good idea to keep an eye on that first sleeper, the one that cost you money. It is bound to awaken at some point, and when it does, it often becomes hyperactive. The longer it has slept, the more likely a candidate it becomes for your prompt attention once it has shown signs of life.

THE 2 TO 1 BETS

Returning to the 12-number combinations, the dozens and columns that pay 2 to 1; trying for one win in five attempts on these can be rewarding and restful at the same time. A few months ago I sat down at a roulette table and began using this progression: 2-4-6-8-12 (risk $32) on dozens and columns that had slept through four or five spins. (At any given time there is almost always at least one of these available.) To my surprise, I won about $100 in an hour and one-half. In the process I'm sure I must have lost my little series of $32 two or three times, but I never went beyond the top bet of $12 and I never repeated a series on a losing sleeper. On average, any given column or dozen can be expected to sleep 10 spins or more once in every 170 spins, but if you're betting only on those which have already slept through five or six spins, you know that ratio is bound to be much lower than 170 to 1.

For faster action with fairly limited risk, your running record of prior spins will often show you at least one column and one dozen, both of which have slept four or more spins simultaneously. Bet on both of them using a bet series like this:

1-2-3-5-8 (risk $19)

Waiting for five-spin sleepers will improve the safety factor considerably, but it will also slow the action. If you do that, you'd have a fair chance of holding your own or better, even if you cut your bet series down to four bets. With the above sample series, that would reduce risk on a single sleeper to $11. Final warning: resist any temptation to continue to bet a column or dozen on which you have lost your series, until after it has had at least one win.

EVEN-CHANCE SLEEPERS

Exactly the same principle applies to these as to the odds propositions I've been discussing. The main differences are: (1) the progressions can be shorter since these are (approximately) even-money bets; (2) the rate of bet escalation must be steeper since no odds are paid; and (3) "sleeping" time can be as little as three spins, though four is safer.

I have frequently bet against any even proposition that had won three times in a row, using a simple Martingale such as 5-10-20. Though I've not recorded my results, it seems safe to say that I've won more often than I've lost, but my typical losses have been larger than my typical winnings. While this approach can be enjoyable, it tends to lull one into a sense of false security and I suspect that it would lose in the long run. If one confines his bets to four-spin sleepers, his patience may occasionally be taxed, but I believe he'll have fair chance of winning on balance provided he always limits his bets to a three-stage Martingale-type progression.

LABOUCHERE

You'll recall this as the famous system that originated with roulette as played on the French Riviera. In it you start with a series of from two to five numbers totaling the amount you will win after you've cancelled out all of your losses. You always bet the total of the two outside numbers in your bet series. Every lost bet adds just one number to your series, and every win cancels two numbers. Therefore, you must eventually come out ahead if you win slightly more than one-third of your bets — and if you don't run into the house limit first.

As I've already indicated, this system will usually produce a lot of small profits, but it is very dangerous. With a run of losses, bets accelerate with astonishing speed, almost frightening when viewed in relation to the amount one is trying to win. Basically it is a bad system unless it is handled with consummate discretion.

With Labouchere, I believe the most discreet action you can take is to stop whenever your net loss in a single series reaches a fixed point, say 10 times the unit profit you're trying for. The loss should be treated as one game in a set of tennis or one inning in a baseball game.

Suppose you want a unit profit of $6; a conservative series then might be 1-1-2-2 or 1-2-1-2. With such a series, you should have a fairly good chance of winning 10 times or more for each time you reached the $60 pre-set loss limit — especially if you bet only even-chance sleepers, limiting yourself to one win and a maximum of three bets per sleeper. Any even chance that has not shown in three spins, or even two spins, would qualify for this system. If you wish to try Labouchere without the bother of recording all spins, then either of the bet-selection procedures in Chapter 2 may prove an acceptable alternative to betting on sleepers.

No question but that Labouchere is a lot of fun to use — especially when it's winning — but my parting words on it have to be if you can find a place where it can be played with 10¢ or 25¢ chips, by all means play it there. Or better yet, if you find such a place where the house limit on even chances is at least 2,000 times the smallest permitted bet ($500 with 25¢ chips) that might be an ideal place in which to experiment with *Reverse Labouchere* as described in Chapter 5.

PARLAYS

A most relaxing and often rewarding way to play roulette. Remember the Englishman who did so by betting all six of the even chances at the same time? Well, here's one on the same order, but on a very small scale. Recently I walked up to a roulette table just to pass the time and rest. I bought twenty $1 chips and bet one of them on odds. My plan was to try for four consecutive parlays (five successive wins). My stack of chips was only about half depleted when there came a series of odd numbers and I had my five consecutive wins, enabling me to pocket $31 profit on a $1 bet.

Betting as I did in that instance, I probably averaged one new chip on the table every second spin, but if one wanted to accelerate his chance of catching a winning parlay, he could do so by risking just one chip per spin. He would then bet on both odd and even, or red and black, and of course after each spin he'd have one winner and one loser — unless a zero came up. He'd replace the losing chip and let the winning bet ride. Doing this, if he were lucky enough to hit a run of seven or eight straight, he would win $127 or $255 with his $1 bet — but keep in mind that he would have been investing at the rate of $70 to $90 per hour.

I do not recommend the use of anything like the 6-number parlay progression described in Chapter 6. That progression seems to do well in craps — and it might do well in roulette in the very long run, but in a short period there would be too much risk of losses being lumped together.

Parlays can be tempting when you've just won a bet on a group of numbers that has had a long "sleep." Whereas an even-money parlay would win 3 to 1, the parlay payout on a 2 to 1 proposition would be 8 to 1, and it would be 80 to 1 on an 8 to 1 bet such as a four-number "final," or 143 to 1 on a three-number "final." (Note: I've seen an 11 repeat so often at the crap tables that I hesitate to deprecate these long-shot bets, but the odds they pay speak for themselves. An 11 parlayed for $1 would return a $239 profit with a 15 to 1 payout.)

A safer way of employing the parlay principle is to escalate bets as you win, drawing down a part of each win after the second one. This would be exactly the same procedure as the "straight-up" method previously discussed. You might, for example, plan to use a winning-bet series like this:

5-10-15-25-40

Your initial bet of $5 would be your only risk. You would recover that $5 after your second win, another $5 after your third win, and $10 after your fourth win. If you won all five bets, you'd be ahead $95 — but of course, if you had parlayed that original $5, you'd have won $155.

EVEN-CHANCE PROGRESSIONS

Although I like parlays and betting on sleepers, I suspect that one's chances of winding up in the plus column would be better if he used a system such as Step Ladder (p. 85), in which winning bets were escalated slowly enough so that the loss of three or even four bets after he was well along in his bet series would not have to wipe out all his profit. This could be accomplished by modifying my previously suggested procedures for that system, as follows:

There need be no change in the bet series or in the initial program of moving up one when you win and down one when you lose. However, from plus 8 on up, you would have to win twice the amount of any bet before advancing in the series. In other words, before moving to the next higher rung, you would have to win 8 twice with no loss, or four times if you lost it twice. Then, if you were to lose three times the amount you were betting at any level beyond 8, you would still have a net profit on that series, and a reasonable option of backing down one or two rungs and continuing the same series or starting a new series. Playing this way, your profit after a double win at the 12 level would be in the $70 to $75 area, more than enough to cushion three or four losses at the next rung of the ladder.

Because of the serious threat posed by the two zeros, it is unwise in roulette to chase losses very far with increasing bets. On a partnership basis, the Double-Win and the "2-5" progressions might perform passably, but when you consider that a zero would cause both partners to lose at the same time it is difficult to become too enthusiastic. Certainly, any bet series of that type should be limited to no more than five or six bets.

You will probably find, as I have, that as a rule systems calling for minimum risk relative to the amounts that can be won are the ideal prescriptions for this game — at least on this side of the Atlantic. Such systems include:

1. Trying for four or more consecutive parlays on the even chances;
2. Using conservative progressions to bet on "sleepers," especially columns, dozens, and finals; and
3. "Step Ladder" using the conservative formula outlined above.

Table 13 shows a couple of examples of what I regard as

TABLE 13
Conservative Progressions for 3- and 4-number Combinations

Finals 0 to 6 (pay 8:1):		Finals 7 to 9 (pay 11:1):	
Bet ($)	Net profit	Bet (25¢ chips)	Net profit
1	8	3	8.25
1	7	3	7.50
1	6	3	6.75
2	13	6	14.25
2	11	6	12.75
2	9	6	11.25
3	15	6	9.75
3	12	9	16.50
4	17	9	14.25
4	13	9	12.00
5	17	9	9.75
28.00 Risk		12	15.75
		12	12.75
		12	9.75
		26.25 Risk	

"conservative" progressions. These could be used on the 8 to 1 and 11 to 1 "finals," or any other three- or four-number combinations, and the betting would be done with 25¢ chips.

As for the timing of these or any other progressions — when to begin one — please refer to Table 11 on page 146. If, as I have suggested, you jot down the numbers as they come up, in three vertical columns on the pad in front of you, you'll not find it hard to spot sleepers that may be ripe for the plucking.

Talking about "conservative" progressions or systems reminds me of something that happened a few years ago. A friend phoned to ask my opinion of a system he'd picked up in a magazine article. The article advised readers to write down their guesses for each of the even chances in roulette for the six spins immediately following. Then they were to bet as they had guessed, using a straight six-stage Martingale. They would bet 1 2 4 8 16 32, so a win at any point in the series would net $1 on each of the three sets of even chances.

The article explained that the odds were 63 to 1 that they would not be wrong on six consecutive guesses, so they would be virtually sure to win $3 every four to six spins of the wheel, or about $50 per hour. It concluded with a punch line to the effect that all Nevada casinos welcome system players with a sneer, but their attitude will change when "you walk away with their cash."

Well, $3 every five or six spins isn't to be sneered at — but what about the $192 investment needed to win that $3? The laws of chance say that if you played long enough, you would break even were it not for those two zeros. They also tell you that it would be quite possible for you to lose that $64 series three or four times in the course of an hour's play.

I believe the likelihood of missing any even bet six times in a row is far too great to justify risking $64 to win $1. In fact, it is seldom advisable to bet 63 to 1 on anything — even if you believe the chances are 100 to 1 in your favor.

Remember the Truman-Dewey campaign for the Presidency in 1948. I knew a cautious and conservative gentleman who at that time owned a list of stocks worth perhaps a bit more than $100,000. He feared that if Truman won, the market would drop sharply and that he might suffer a substantial loss. So he decided that he'd like a little insurance if he could get it on favorable terms. Dewey was an overwhelming favorite to win the election and the papers were quoting 20 to 1 odds and more. Through his broker, this concerned investor was able to place $3,000 on Truman on the floor of the New York Stock Exchange, at 15 to 1 odds. You know what happened; Truman won and his victory cost one of the members of the Exchange a cool $45,000. Moral: it's almost always better to be on the receiving end of very long odds.

THE 35 TO 1 SYSTEM

We now come to the only system specifically designed for roulette that I have ever heard of, that seems to win on balance against a double-zero wheel.

This system is based on what is sometimes called the "law of unequal distribution." Applied to a social group, that law dictates that one person at the top of a pyramid-like structure will have most of the money or power; two persons next to the top will be almost as potent, but way down at the base of the pyramid we'll find 50,000 sad specimens who don't have much of anything. Remember the old saw, "The rich get richer and the poor get children."

In roulette that same law tells us that during a fixed and limited period we can never expect anything like even distribution of the slots into which the little ball slides. The odds against hitting 38 different numbers in 38 successive spins would be absolutely staggering. To hit as many as 25 different slots in 38 spins would be quite a feat. This means, of course, that while some numbers are hit two, three, four, or more times, others will be completely neglected.

To me the fascinating thing about this is that at any given point, those numbers that have been coming up most frequently have a strange tendency to keep right on doing the same thing — at least for a while.

Okay, what is the best way to capitalize on this phenomenon? Obviously, there are quite a few plausible procedures that could be profitable if the underlying premise proved sound. The procedure I am about to describe is the product of trial and error experimenting, and if it's not the best, perhaps you will be able to improve on it.

Stand back of any roulette layout and clock each number that comes up in a notebook. All the numbers from zero to 36 should be listed in a vertical column at the left side of one page. After 15 to 30 spins, one of those numbers will have been hit three times — and that is when you go into action.

You begin by betting on that number. Your plan is to bet on that number plus as many as four of the next numbers to get three hits each, unless before you have five working numbers you have already won a predetermined amount and ended that game.

With each spin you bet the same amount on each of your numbers until one of them comes up, or until you've lost 25 to 30 successive times on an individual number. In the latter case you stop betting on that number and resume only if and when it gets another hit while the same game is in progress. If you had five working numbers when you blocked it out, do not replace it with a new number. You never have more than five different numbers to bet on in a single game.

In your notebook to the right of your column of 38 numbers, you write in the numbers you're playing, and you keep track of your losing bets under each number with a series of five lines like this: ~~1111~~

When you win on a number, the amount of your bet on that number should be increased from 50 percent to 100 percent, and if you win a second time on the same number, you again raise your bet, this time to an amount equal to the total of your first two smaller bets. Thus your bet series might be 1-2-3, 2-3-5, or 3-5-8. The increases presuppose that your first win on a number does not give you enough net profit to meet your minimum objective for a single game. When said objective has been met, you cash in your chips and look for another table.

Now let's consider profit objectives and the amounts you're going to risk to attain those objectives. Your stake for each game should be no more than four times the amount of a win on your smallest bet. Thus, if that bet were $1, you should be prepared to risk no more than four times $35, or $140 on that game. If your small bet were $3, your "bank" for that game would be $400 or $420. Your initial minimum profit objective in each game should be about 30 times your small bet — and that minimum objective will decline as losses eat into your "bank."

Divide your "bank" into four equal parts. If your bank is $140, you segregate $35 of chips, and as long as you're working on that first $35, your objective will be at least $30 of net profit. If a hit before that $35 is exhausted gives you a net profit of only $10, the game continues and that first one-fourth of your "bank" will have been expanded to $45 while your minimum profit objective remains unchanged.

When you are into the second quarter of your "bank," your profit objective shrinks to 20 times your small bet — and if a win at that stage doesn't meet that objective but reduces your net investment in the game to less than $35, you are back in your first quarter with your original $30 profit objective.

In your third quarter, any win that enables you to break about even should end the game — and when you're working on the last quarter of your "bank," your game ends either when you get your first hit or when your chips are all gone, whichever happens first.

You'll find that your average profit per winning game is materially greater than these minimum objectives, and that in about half your losing games, net losses will be considerably less than your "bank." As a very rough estimate, I'd say that you would generally break even or better if you win three games for each one you lose. You should do better than that.

When I first stumbled onto this strange system, my excitement knew no bounds. On my good little home set I won 14 successive games before my first loss. Then I won about seven more games. Then I turned the system over to a friend who is with one of the major aerospace companies and who has his own computer at home. He reported that in 30,000 spins on his computer, the win-loss ratio was an amazing 16 to 1.

It all seemed too good to be true, and I regret having to inform you that a 4 or 5 to 1 win ratio is actually about as much as one can reasonably hope for. Further testing has convinced me of that. The computer must have been improperly programmed — or its random numbers weren't truly random.

Now a few words of caution. If you try this system it will be difficult for you not to attract attention for two reasons. First, the money you'll be using and betting will be conspicuous since most of the other chips on the table will be of the 25¢ variety and your bets will represent more risk for the house than most. This could be so even if your betting scale were only $1, $2, $3. Incidentally, if you improvise your own progression, don't forget to adjust profit objectives up or down so that they bear roughly the same relationships to the size of your bets, as those suggested above.

Another factor that may set you apart from other players is the obvious fact that you're using a system, and even worse, it's a system that seems to win. That will definitely attract the attention of pit bosses who are likely to conclude that any system that wins, regardless of the amounts, represents a clear and present danger to their employer.

Nevada courts have ruled that casinos can deal or refuse to deal to anyone for any reason. Accordingly, you run the risk of being barred and perhaps having your name circulated among other casinos, once they've concluded that whatever you're doing is not likely to benefit them now or later on.

To avoid embarrassment and possible blacklisting, I suggest the following steps:

1. Pick your spots carefully — only active tables preferably where there are bets bigger than those you propose to make.
2. Never play more than one series at a table during the same eight-hour shift. When you change tables, it is best to change casinos as well.
3. When any one of your numbers hits, try to act surprised.

To this point my comments upon the performance to be expected of this system have assumed an honest wheel with truly random numbers coming up. It is safe to assume that most Nevada wheels are honest, but there is another serious factor to be considered. There are two schools of opinion as to the amount of control dealers have over roulette spins. One holds that they have little or no control and that they attempt none. The other is convinced that most dealers can come within five or six slots of any point on the wheel whenever they wish. My own experience suggests that some of them, but by no means all, do have a considerable measure of "expertise."

The notebook you'll want to use for this system should open up vertically so that there's length enough to list the 38 numbers in a single column. In that notebook you might also make a diagram showing all the numbers exactly as they are placed on the wheel. The diagram should be in the shape of a square with the zero and 8 numbers on top, the double zero and 8 numbers on the bottom, and 10 numbers on each side. As you watch the play before making your own first bet, your diagram may help you to spot and avoid any dealer who seems able to consistently "call his shots."

When you find yourself in a contest with a dealer who apparently has the skill and the desire to beat you, your choices are limited. You can, of course, quit and go elsewhere, or before he spins you might try placing your bets on the numbers on the betting layout immediately adjacent to the numbers you plan to bet on — either one digit lower or higher than your real numbers. Then, as soon as he spins the little ball, move those bets to their proper places. You would not be permitted to do that in Europe or England, but in the United States players are allowed to place or change their bets at any time before the dealer says, "no more bets" — usually 5 to 10 seconds after the little ball begins to go "round and round."

To give you a rough idea of the kind of distribution you might expect in a "fair" game, I have the record of 82 spins at one of the tables in the Stardust Hotel in Las Vegas. In that series, one number came up seven times, 2 five times, 3 four times and 5 numbers did not show at all. I would call that distribution fairly typical.

When tabulating results at a table before making your first bet, it is well to keep in mind that your prospects of a fast profit vary inversely with the evenness of the distribution of numbers hit. You want those numbers to be as unevenly distributed as possible. At the beginning, if you have 12 or 15 numbers with two hits apiece before any number has come up three times, the risk of a slow or possibly a losing game is heightened.

Before attempting to use this system in casino play, I suggest you re-read the instructions, making special note of the points at which you should end each series, as well as the various precautions I've emphasized. You should also be clear as to the amounts of your expected average win — roughly 35 times your smallest bet, also the maximum risk in a single game — about four times the amount you can win on your smallest bet. Thus, if your bet progression were 2-3-5, your average win per series should be close to $70, with your "bank" or loss limit at $280.

Good luck — and do your best to prevent prying eyes from seeing those pages in your notebook. Remember also that there are other systems good enough to produce small profits at roulette — and that if one exercises care and discretion in choosing and implementing his method of play, roulette can be a truly enjoyable pastime.

CHAPTER 13

Blackjack (21)

Blackjack or 21 is essentially a game of skill. In the United States it is unquestionably the most popular of all casino games — excluding slot machines — and it is also the number one contributor to casino profits. To the uninitiated the game appears deceptively simple.

21 tables usually seat just six players, and the dealers, one for each table, stand facing the players behind the table. Nowadays many dealers are young girls who generally are well trained and a bit faster on average in the performance of their dealing functions than their male counterparts.

The ostensible object of the game is to be dealt only as many cards as are needed to give one a count as near as possible to 21 without going over that number. Tens and face cards count as 10 and all other cards except aces count their face value. Aces count as either 1 or 11 at the player's option, but for the dealer they count as 11 unless that would put him over 21, in which case they count as 1.

Bets are made before any cards are dealt. Then two cards are dealt to each player and the dealer, one of whose cards is dealt face up for all to see. After that the dealer offers each player in turn a chance to exercise his option of standing pat or taking a "hit." If he chooses to be "hit" he can draw as many cards as he pleases, but if he goes over 21, he is required to announce that fact at once. The player has two additional options that he must announce before he takes a hit; he can "double down" or, if his first two cards are a pair, he can split the pair playing each card as the first card of a separate hand. These last two options almost always involve a doubling of the player's original bet.

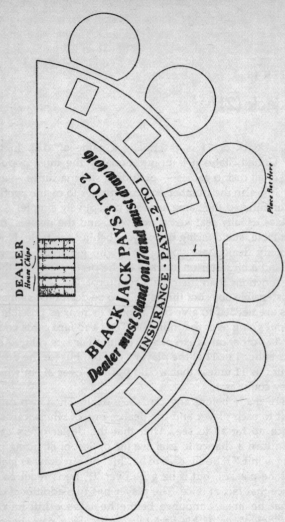

BLACK JACK PAYS 3 TO 2
Dealer must stand on 17 and must draw to 16
INSURANCE · PAYS · 2 TO 1

DEALER
House Chips

Place Bet Here

THE BLACKJACK TABLE

A small minority of casinos give players a third option, which is to "surrender." When surrendering is permitted, a player who feels that there is a better than 2 to 1 chance that he'll lose a hand, may elect instead to give up half his bet and not play the hand at all.

You may have noticed that I said the "ostensible" objective was to come as close to 21 as possible without going over. The *real objective* of each player is simply to *beat the dealer* who must play his own hand mechanically according to a fixed set of rules prescribed by the casino. He has no options whatever. In Nevada there is only one significant variation (that I know of) in the rules governing dealers' play. They all have to draw to 16 and about half of them stand on any 17, while the other half must stand on a "hard" 17 but must draw to a "soft" 17.

In Blackjack parlance a soft hand is one containing an ace that may be counted either as 11 or 1. Thus, an A,6 held by a player is a soft hand which may be counted as either 7 or 17. A dealer with that holding has a "soft" 17. If he were required to hit that soft 17 and drew an 8, for example, he would then have a "hard" 15 — a hand in which the ace had to be counted as 1. With 15, he would, of course, have to draw again and risk going over 21 and "busting."

The major determinants of a player's action after he has received his first two cards are: (1) his own holding; and (2) the dealer's exposed card. There is also a third factor of great importance, namely, the makeup of the cards remaining to be dealt. If high cards predominate, that favors the players since they, unlike the dealer, are never required to draw to a "stiff" — a hand with a count of 12 to 16 which might "bust" if a single additional card were drawn. This matter of the undealt cards will be discussed in depth later on, but for now let's assume that the only things we know and have to know are:

1. Our own two cards.
2. The dealer's exposed card.
3. We play before the dealer, who always plays last, and if we "bust" (go over 21) we lose regardless of what the dealer does.

4. If we have a blackjack (ace plus any 10-count card) as our first two cards, we must announce that fact at once, and we'll be paid one and one-half times our bet unless the dealer also has one. In that case, we'll "push" (tie).

5. If the dealer's up-card is a 10 or a face card, he will glance at his hole card and announce his blackjack if he has one, before resuming the deal. If he hasn't a blackjack, there is a 7 to 5 probability that he has a count of 17 to 20 and will not have to draw.

6. If the dealer's up-card is an ace, he'll ask if we wish to take "insurance" (against his having a blackjack). The "insurance" bet is one-half the amount of our original bet that the dealer *does* have a 10-count card under his ace. If we make that bet and win it, we'll be paid 2 to 1 odds on it, but we'll only break even on that deal because we'll lose our original bet unless we also have a blackjack.

7. Of the 52 cards in the deck, 16, or just less than one-third, are 10-count, while there are just four each of all the other denominations.

Each time the cards are shuffled and there is a new deal, these seven factors are essentially all we have to go on when we make our decision as to standing, hitting, doubling down, splitting, or surrendering. In a single-deck game with four to six players, 50 percent of all deals are likely to be new deals. In a double-deck game 14 percent to 20 percent of the deals will be new deals, and there will be no real basis for deviating from basic strategy in at least 25 percent of the other deals. One can assume, therefore, that about 50 percent of all his blackjack decisions will be more or less routine; that on those hands there will be no reason to depart from what might be called "basic strategy."

BASIC STRATEGY

Most authorities tell you that their recommendations are based on extensive computer tests, pure mathematics, or a combination of both. Yet their findings are by no means consistent. Since I have studied Thorp, Revere, Wilson, and Roberts, as well as Scarne, Riddle, and others — and have played hundreds of hours of casino blackjack — I am not certain as to the origin of my own theories and policies. I prefer simply to ascribe them to a great deal of fairly successful experience plus a lot of reading on the subject. (You will learn later on why I feel obliged to qualify my success story with the word "fairly.") In any case, Tables 14 through 17 contain my prescriptions for winning blackjack under *average or normal* conditions.

DOUBLING DOWN

Whenever, based on your first two cards and the dealer's up-card, you feel that after drawing one more card you will have a better than even chance of beating the dealer, you are permitted to double your bet or to increase it by any amount up to 100 percent. To do so, however, you must give up the privilege of drawing more than one additional card, and must stand on whatever card is dealt to you. This is a most important privilege and places that limit it to hard hands only, or to 10s and 11s only, as some do, should be avoided.

In the long run it is not possible to overcome the dealer's enormous advantage of playing last and winning all previously "busted" hands, unless your winning bets are decisively bigger than your losing bets. There are four types of situations that call for increasing the size of your bets. These are: (1) doubling down; (2) pair splitting; (3) a favorable deck — one rich in high cards, especially 10s and aces; and (4) the "insurance" option on certain occasions. Knowing when to double down and doing it each time conditions are favorable is essential. Basic doubling down strategy is shown in Table 15.

PAIR SPLITTING

Favorable pair-splitting opportunities are often overlooked by experienced 21 players who question the wisdom of exchanging one poor hand for two poor hands, when doing so means doubling their risk. The controlling factor should almost always be the dealer's exposed card. When that card

TABLE 14
Basic Standing and Hitting Strategy (Single Deck)

Dealer shows	Hard hands stand on:	Soft hands stand on:
2	13	18*
3	13	18*
4–6	12	18*
7, 8	17	18
9	17	19
10	17	19
Ace	17	18

*Refer to Table 15, Basic Doubling Down Strategy

is a 3, 4, 5, or 6, an expert player will split any pair in the deck except 5s and 10s — and possibly 4s if the deck is rich and he prefers to double down on his 4s.

The only pair that should never be split is 5s, while the one pair that should always be split is aces. Eights should be split almost always, while 10s should hardly ever be split. Incidentally, I trust that you understand that a 10 and a face card would be a pair since they both count as 10 — and that in this text wherever reference is made to "10s," face cards are included. In the case of 8s and 10s, the exceptions to the usual practice would apply only to a very rich deck. In that circumstance one should surrender his 8s against a 9 or 10 if possible; otherwise he should stand. Under the same circumstances, one would be justified in splitting 10s against a dealer's 5 or 6. This last play would doubtless evoke some caustic comments from one's fellow players, but rest assured that it is an excellent percentage play.

Aces are a special case. When they are split you will be dealt just two cards, one for each ace, and that will end the hand for you. Even if one of those two cards is another ace, you will not be allowed to split it, as you usually can with any other split pair. As I may have mentioned earlier, each split card is

TABLE 15
Basic Doubling Down Strategy (Single Deck)

Dealer shows	Hard hands double on	Soft hands double on
2, 3	9–11	A6*
4–6	9–11**	A2 to A7***
7	10–11	no
8, 9	10, 11	no
10, A	11	no

*Also A7 vs. 3
** 8 – 11 if deck is very rich
***Also A8 vs. 6

played as a separate hand, the player duplicating his original bet on the second hand, and, except for split aces, drawing as many or as few cards for each hand as he pleases.

A few casinos, but not many, will permit doubling down on a split hand after the first card has been dealt to it. For example, you split your 3s and the first card dealt to one of those 3s is a 7, giving that hand a count of 10. The dealer's up-card is a 5, so you have a prime doubling situation — if they'll allow it. When you sit down at a new table, it is a good idea to inquire about policy on this; and if the policy is affirmative, to be alert for these triple-profit situations.

If, as a result of splitting aces or face cards, you should wind up with one or more blackjacks, don't expect to be paid the usual 1½ to 1 odds. Blackjacks that come that way are synthetic — so they're simply counted as 21 and paid off at even money.

When you study Table 16, you may wonder about the sanity of splitting 8s against a dealer's 9, 10, or ace. The idea of doubling your risk on a poor hand against what appears to be a good hand is not too appealing. But if you do split, the laws of probability will be on your side. Of course you will lose on balance either way, but you'll lose less by splitting.

TABLE 16
Basic Pair Splitting Strategy (Single Deck)

Split	Dealer's up card	Remarks
Aces	anything	always
10s	seldom*	*only vs. dealer's 4 to 6 if deck is *very* rich
9s	2–6, 8, 9	
8s	anything*	*surrender vs. 9 or 10
7s	2–8	surrender vs. 9 and 10 unless deck very poor
6s	2–6	
5s	never	
4s	4–6*	*split with poor deck; double down otherwise
3s	4–7	
2s	3–7	

INSURANCE

When the dealer has an ace up, he'll ask if anyone wants "insurance." What he's really asking is, "Would any of you suckers like to make a side bet of half the amount of your original bet that I've got a 10 or a face card under that ace?" If you make that side bet and win, he'll pay you 2 to 1 odds on that bet, but of course, he'll collect your other bet unless you too have a blackjack. If you lose the so-called "insurance" bet, the hand will be played out normally and you may win your regular bet or lose that one also.

The insurance proposition should be regarded as an extra bet on which the house usually, but not always, has a decided edge — often as much as 15 percent. When insurance is offered you can see at least three cards — your own two plus the dealer's ace. If you had not kept track of the 10s dealt previously and/or if this were a fresh deal, your only guide to the correct odds on that bet would be the ratio of visible 10s to the total number of cards you had seen on that particular deal. Those true odds are shown in Table 17.

Thus, insurance has to be an unattractive proposition when you've seen only three cards and haven't counted 10s. If you've

TABLE 17
Insurance Odds That Dealer's Hole Card Is Not a 10

| Total cards seen | 10-count cards seen: | | | | |
	None	One	Two	Three	Four
3	33:16	34:15	35:14		
5	31:16	32:15	33:14	34:14	35:12
7	29:16	30:15	31:14	32:13	33:12

seen four or more cards with no 10s, or seven cards with only one 10, it may be a fair or even a good bet.

If you happen to have a blackjack and have announced it when insurance is offered, your neighbors and the dealer may advise you to take it, pointing out that by so doing, you guarantee yourself a profit on the hand. If you lose your side bet, you'll receive 1½ to 1 odds on your blackjack. If you win the side bet, the payout is at 2 to 1, while you and the dealer "push" (tie) on your two blackjacks. So in either case you will have won the amount of your original bet, but you may have sacrificed an additional 50 percent profit on that bet. Insurance is never a good bet when the percentages are definitely with the house. In a borderline case it is not illogical to base your "taking" or "refusing" decision on the quality of your own hand. With a good hand such as 19, 20, or 11, the added commitment required can make some sense, but that would not be the case if your hand was one that was likely to lose in any event. To summarize, when in doubt, decline "insurance."

MONEY MANAGEMENT

Your regular (standard) bet should not, as a rule, be more than two and one-half to four percent of your stake. Actually, two percent is enough until you've accumulated some profit. Your maximum bet should be limited to no more than two and one-half to three times your regular bet, which means that it could be as much as six times your normal bet when you double down or split pairs after making a maximum bet. Suppose, for example, your starting stake is $200. Your normal bet should be $5. You could then fall back to $3 when the deck was poor, while with a very favorable deck you might have as much as $30 riding on a doubled-down or split hand.

Resist any inclination you may feel to raise the level of your bets when losing. In this game — as in others — winning and losing streaks can be quite lengthy, and often the best anti-dote for an adverse run is changing tables. I suggest that when-ever you lose four of your first five hands at a new table or as much as 20 percent of your stake at any one table, that you pick up your chips and find another spot to play.

Your betting unit can be increased when you've won at least 30 percent to 40 percent of your original stake. If you begin with a 2½ percent unit bet and continue to win, that ratio can be increased to a maximum of three percent. Thus, with a $500 bankroll, your standard bet might be $15 and you could have as much as $75 riding on a single hand.

There used to be a blackjack school in Long Beach, Califor-nia, that claimed it could teach anyone how to win 100 percent of the time. In essence, its program for winning involved nothing more than elementary play plus a fancy geometric progression in which losing bets would grow in size so fast that if one lost eight or nine consecutive hands and won on the tenth hand, he would be in the clear. Of course, his winning, if any, would be tiny compared with the substantial loss he risked when he made that tenth bet.

I have experienced 9 or 10 consecutive losses at 21 any number of times, but not long ago I may have earned a place in the *Guinness Book of World Records*. Fortunately, I was only playing for supper money — $2 and $3 bets, but believe it or not, I suffered through 16 successive deals without a single win; 15 losses and one "push." Because my bets were so small, I disregarded my own policy of leaving any table where I'd had four or more losses in a row. I tell you this so that you'll be forewarned if you are ever tempted by advertised promises of sure-fire profits at 21 the "easy way — no counting, no calculating, no problem too involved for a 12-year-old." Pure fantasy, you may be absolutely certain.

There are other more sophisticated blackjack schools scattered around the country, from Los Angeles to Las Vegas to Boston. One such, headquartered in Vegas, has branches in six or seven cities and currently charges $595 for 12 hours of group instruction plus follow-up testing. Its pupils are taught the skill elements for the game with emphasis on basic strategy, counting and money management. There is another outfit, in Joliet, Illinois, that charges $795 for its three-day weekends of personal instruction or $295 for its home study courses. If these charges seem high, consider the bait held out to prospective students—astronomical daily earnings, lives of luxury and ease, world travel on the house, once they've completed the courses.

Actually, no amount of instruction or study can assure the average player of anything more than an improvement in his playing skills and in his *chance* to overcome the odds against him when he sits down at a 21 table. The average player is ill-equiped to cope successfully with the various highly effective measures adopted by casinos in recent years to protect themselves against truly expert players. Nevertheless, by judiciously varying the size of his bets, a fairly good player should be able to win considerably more in an average session than he loses on average and to hold his own against the house in at least 40 to 45 percent of his attempts.

We have already touched on the matter of changing the size of bets as the conditions of each deal change. Now let's briefly consider other conditions under which bets might be varied so as to materially affect one's profit (or loss).

I don't know any type of progression that is perfectly adapted to 21. The favorability or unfavorability of the deck changes from deal to deal and there is no way to synchronize those changes with a programmed series of increasing or decreasing bets. However, one can boost his chance for sizeable profits by parlaying winning bets when the deck is favorable. Even if his unusually large parlayed bets attract the unwanted attention of pit bosses, they will not necessarily stamp him as a card counter, since parlays are frequently attempted by every type of player, including the "uninitiated."

Another strategy for a big win is to gradually step up the level of all one's bets, regardless of one's profit or loss position. If you do this, best policy is to pull back sharply after each really good win. This, of course, is risky, but with luck it can serve its purpose. It is a sort of "go for broke" procedure. I do not as a rule advocate escalating losing bets in blackjack, but when one is ahead it's an entirely different matter. If you have already added 10 or 15 percent to your bankroll, chasing losses may slightly reduce the probability of your winding up a winner in that particular session, but if your goal is rapid acceleration or profit, this is one way you might achieve it.

In case you are not sure how to determine whether the deck is favorable or unfavorable, that subject will be discussed in depth in the next chapter. You will be introduced to what I believe are the easiest and most effective card counting systems extant for the game of 21.

If you become an expert player and a consistent winner, do whatever you can to hide those facts. Make your play appear to be haphazard; pocket some of your chips surreptitiously, and when you leave a table change your chips into larger denominations. Then when you go to the window to cash them, cash some of them but not all. Later on when you return to cash the rest of your chips, the cashier will assume that your chips represent new money that you've put into the game. Above all, when your chips on the table are depleted, don't reach into your pocket or purse for more chips. Instead, hand the dealer some new money and let him think that you haven't been doing as well as he'd imagined. All of this, of course, applies only if you are in fact a winning player who hopes to continue doing business with that particular casino.

BASIC STRATEGY SUMMARIZED

Memorizing the standing, doubling, and splitting recommendations as tabulated above should not be too time consuming. When you have done that, you will have gone far toward neutralizing the casino's normal advantage. That would be true even if you used nothing but "flat" bets — each bet the same amount.

Be very leery about "insurance" bets. Make them only when you are certain that the unseen cards have a better-than-normal percentage of 10s and face cards.

What to do when you do not count the cards as they are exposed, or haven't paid close attention to them? If you've seen about 20 cards with only four 10s and no aces, you know that the rest of the deck is rich in these cards and favorable for the player. Increased bets are therefore in order. Just under one-third (31 percent) of the cards in a fresh deck are 10-count, so when you've seen more 10-count cards than three out of 10 or six out of 20, you know that the undealt deck contains less than a normal share of these cards, and you proceed cautiously with small bets.

Remember that no matter how well you play, long-range the house is sure to win more than 50 percent of all hands. Therefore, to win you must increase your bets when the deck is favorable, and double down and split pairs whenever the situation calls for one of those actions. Your average win must be materially larger than your average loss.

Lastly, a rather touchy subject — "common sense versus basic strategy" as outlined here or in any other writing. All rules are made to be broken on occasion. The books says to stand on 17, and your own two (or three) cards add up to 15. However, 15 of the last 20 cards dealt have ranged from 2 to 7. Forget the book and stand. Or, knowing the deck to be very rich in high cards, you hold 14 against the dealer's 10. The low card in your hand further reduced the proportion of low cards remaining to be dealt. Again, forget the book and sit tight. The dealer's chance of having a low hole card is exactly equal to your chance of drawing a small card, but remember, if you both "bust," he wins.

Cold logic will also tell you to deviate at times when you face what would normally be a sound doubling or splitting situation. Suppose you hold a pair of 9s against the dealer's anything, knowing that the balance of the deck consists almost entirely of low cards. Obviously, it would be ridiculous to split your pair. Or, in the same circumstance, you could have 10 against the dealer's 7 or 8. Again, forget the book and don't double down. It seldom pays to ignore common sense.

There are millions of possible card combinations. To cope with some of them, judgment often is a better tool than fallible memory, provided always that one's judgment is backed by a solid grounding in fundamentals. That grounding is what this chapter is all about.

CHAPTER 14

Card Counting in Blackjack

I n the preceding chapter there were many references to the composition of the deck, the makeup of the undealt cards, and especially the ratio of 10s and aces to low cards. The difference between a good 21 player and an expert is the latter's ability to count, plus his willingness to apply the required effort and concentration. There is absolutely no doubt that in an honest game a real expert has a definite edge over the casino. This is particularly true in Nevada, where the rules, though they differ from casino to casino, are generally the most liberal to be found anywhere.

However, in most if not all Nevada casinos, "counting" is a dirty word. Counters are frequently barred, and by some sort of twisted logic, they have even been lumped in with cheaters and other undesirables in certain Las Vegas, Reno, and Tahoe circles.

In Atlantic City counting also is a dirty word, but under current regulations, counters, as such, cannot be barred. So, virtually all casinos there protect themselves against skillful players by using eight-deck shoes, dealing no more than half of each shoe and authorizing their dealers to shuffle at will.

In his recently published book *Your Best Bet*, Mike Goodman, a pit boss in a well-known Vegas casino, specifically classifies counters with cheaters and does so in a manner that I suspect could make him a vulnerable target for a class action lawsuit if blackjack counters ever decided to band together and go after him. He implies that in England and most European countries one would be arrested as a criminal for counting, and he states flatly that Nevada clubs all have access to a "black book" with pictures and descriptions of known cheaters, counters and undesirables.

A current news report tells of a player who, after winning

several thousand dollars at the Hilton Hotel in Las Vegas, was barred as a "counter." The player sued the hotel in the Nevada courts and lost. Undaunted, however, he now plans to appeal his case to the United States Supreme Court. You may be as astonished as I was to learn that he will be represented in the appeal by none other than the A.C.L.U. — the American Civil Liberties Union.

It has been established, I believe, that Nevada clubs can legally bar anyone for any reason, but of course, that does not give them the right to try to stigmatize honest and reputable individuals just because they happen to be skillful enough to win at a game that would produce at least a 10¢ profit for the gambling establishment for every dollar wagered by the public, if only they could make it a game of pure chance.

Card games, including 21 and poker, and even Baccarat, are quite distinct from other casino games in one major respect. As the cards are dealt, the composition of the cards remaining in the deck constantly changes — as do the odds for or against the appearance subsequently of any given card. That being so, the odds in favor of the house or against the player must also change or be reversed as the cards are dealt. Every experienced 21 player knows this, but only a tiny minority do very much about it.

Under typical casino conditions anywhere in the world accurate counting in Blackjack is extremely difficult. Dealers perform their functions at maximum speeds; they bury exposed cards as fast as they can; they conceal cards that should be exposed for all to see, and they reshuffle seemingly at will — often when there are more than enough cards left in the deck for another round or two. Add to this the fact that Nevada clubs for some time have been moving away from the single-deck games to the two-, four- and even the six-deck variety, and you can see that the counter's lot is not an easy one. It is considerably less difficult to keep track of the count in a single-deck game than it is when multiple decks are used.

At this point I'm sure you don't have to be told that counting requires intense and unremitting concentration, but if winning is important to you, it can be well worth the effort.

Blackjack players as a class were probably only dimly aware of the value of keeping track of 10s, aces, and low cards (especially 5s), until 15 or 20 years ago when Professor Edward O. Thorp's best-selling book *Beat The Dealer* hit the market. That book detailed the means by which a truly competent (and gifted) blackjack player could expect to win consistently — unless he were cheated. Nevada gaming people were so shaken by Dr. Thorp's revelations that they changed the rules of the game so as to make it next to impossible for a player to win. However, when they saw their blackjack business drying up, and realized how very few people there were who had the computer-like minds needed to implement Thorp's system, they changed the rules back again. Later, as Revere and others began to develop, publicize, and sell more simplified systems for counting, the casinos retaliated with counter measures of the types mentioned above and others that we'll discuss later; but to date they have shied away from tampering with the basic rules of the game.

COUNTING THEORIES

Most really good blackjack players watch the cards quite closely as they are dealt and played. If they don't actually count, they observe the distribution of high and low cards, hoping of course, to see a lot of low cards and relatively few 10s and aces in the early deals. When the balance of the deck is heavy (rich) in 10-count and other high cards plus aces, the players' chances are materially improved and they should increase the size of their bets.

There are a variety of counting methods, and they all begin with a count or an estimate of the number of cards dealt on each round, telling the counter how many cards remain in the deck(s). He doesn't have to know how far down the dealer will go before his next reshuffle, since his primary concern is the proportion of high cards, 10s, or whatever groups he follows, to all the cards remaining. I should add, however, that dealing right down to the end of the deck or close to it, can be of enormous benefit to an accurate counter. At this writing I understand that several places in the Reno, Tahoe area still do just that, but they compensate in other ways. In Las Vegas dealing down to anywhere near the end of the deck(s) is strictly taboo.

Some experts advocate counting 10s and face cards only. Once that is mastered, they suggest you count aces and then 5s. Fives, of course, are especially valuable for the dealer since they give him a perfect hand when he must draw to 16, and a good hand if he has to draw to any other "stiff." When you've counted these cards along with the other cards dealt, you do a little rapid subtraction and division to determine if they are likely to be more or less plentiful in the next round or the next several rounds and whether you should make a big bet, a medium bet, or a small bet.

Another school of thought holds that knowing the makeup of the remaining cards in terms of cards favorable for the player versus cards favorable for the dealer is the main thing. Besides that, they contend that it is easier to balance off the 20 low cards (2s through 6s) against the 20 high cards (10-count and aces) than it is to count the latter and then do the needed arithmetic. With this balancing system, you need only see how many more cards of either group are dealt on each round and then keep a running count of your plusses and minuses. If two more low cards than high cards appear on the first round, your count is plus two and your next bet should be two units. Of course, a plus two or three count toward the end of a deal would be much more significant than at the start. With this system 7s, 8s, and 9s are considered neutral and are not counted. Some users prefer to treat 3s through 7s as their low group instead of 2s through 6s. They theorize that a 7 is apt to be a more useful card for the dealer than a 2, so they ignore 2s, 8s, and 9s for purposes of their count.

At this point you may be saying to yourself, "How can he imply that aces and 10s aren't favorable for the dealer just as they are for the player?" The answer is that they are. However, if the dealer gets a blackjack, he's paid no odds, while a player's blackjack is worth 150 percent of his bet. If there are two or more players, or if one player is playing two or more hands, the probabilities are 2 to 1 or better that the player(s) will get the blackjack. But the main point relates to the dealer's obligation to draw to any stiff hand. A 10 can't help him, and either a 9 or an ace would be of no use to him on four of the five possible stiffs — 12 to 16. This gives the player a distinct advantage whenever the deck contains a preponderance of high cards. Players and dealers alike have equal chances of drawing stiffs to go in with, but only the dealer has to "hit" a stiff when the odds may be 2 or 3 to 1 that he'll bust.

COUNTING 10s

The most widely used and perhaps the easiest method of estimating the favorability of the undealt cards is known as the "10-count." Tens and face cards are by long odds the most important cards in any game of 21. That is so not only because there are 16 of them, but also because when one is drawn to any "stiff," that hand will "bust" and additionally because every blackjack must include a 10-count card. As the cards are exposed, players who concentrate on these cards equate their appearances either with the total of all cards dealt, or with a corresponding group of 16 low cards.

Since dealers have to draw to any "stiff," a preponderance of low cards is more favorable for them than for the players — and vice versa. The 16 most favorable cards for anyone who must draw to stiffs are either 3s through 6s or 4s through 7's; take your pick. I happen to like 3s through 6s, but either group matches the 10-counts numerically, and in a single-deck game it is relatively easy to balance one group of only 16 cards against another such group.

There are several ways to count these opposing card groups. The most accurate and revealing method is to count each group separately, treating the resulting two numbers as the numerator and the denominator of a fraction. In a single-deck game the fraction you'd begin with would be 16/16ths. The first 16 represents the low cards, while the second 16 represents the 10-count cards. As each card in either group appeared, you would deduct one from the previous total for that group, always thinking of the low-card total as the first part of your fraction and the high-card total as the second part. Thus, if you had seen six low cards and only two high cards, your resulting fraction would be 10/14ths. If the same 3 to 1 ratio prevailed so that later on in the same deal you had seen 12 low cards versus only four high cards, your fraction would then be 4/12ths, an extremely favorable and unlikely "count." In any case, you want that fraction to be as small as possible, and you'll vary the size of your bets accordingly.

When the deck became unfavorable, your fraction would no longer be a "fraction"; it would be more than 16/16ths. For example, if only one low card had appeared against five high cards, said fraction would then have become 15/11ths — quite unfavorable.

An easier but less accurate way of counting the same groups of cards, is to begin at zero adding 1 whenever a low card is exposed, and subtracting 1 for each high card. Then, when the count becomes plus 2 or higher, the deck is favorable; when it's minus 2 or lower, the deck is considered unfavorable.

With this method, the degree of favorability, or its lack, would be indicated by the size of the plus or minus count — and also by the relation of that count to the number of cards remaining to be dealt. In a two-deck game, for example a count of plus 3 after the first deal might indicate that 26 low cards remained in the deck, versus 29 high cards; not an impressively favorable ratio. If, however, only 30 cards remained to be dealt, that same plus 3 count might indicate seven remaining low cards to 10 high cards, a very favorable mix.

HI-LOW DIFFERENTIAL

My own preferred method of "counting" is something I call the "hi-lo differential." On each deal I observe the total number of cards dealt and the total number of 9s, 10s, and aces. I also try to make a mental note of how many 8s I've seen. Suppose in a 20-card deal I've seen seven 9s, 10s, and aces and one 8. I know then that there were twelve 2s through 7s on that deal, and my count is plus 5 (12 minus 7). I also know that the undealt 32 cards include three 8s and 17 high cards versus 12 low cards, an excellent mix for me and a rather poor one for the dealer. In this example I've assumed a single-deck game, so with a count of plus 5, I'd probably make my maximum bet — two and one-half or three times my unit or normal bet.

There are 24 nines through aces, and 24 twos through sevens in a deck, so if you count the high cards plus the 8s, and you know how many cards were dealt, you must, ipso facto, know how many low cards were dealt. You keep a running count of the differential between the high and low groups, and the differential becomes the prime determinant of the size of your bet on the next deal. If low cards have outnumbered the high cards, the remaining deck is favorable and the differential is expressed as a plus. When high cards predominate, the differential becomes a minus, and you make a small bet on the next deal.

To help you see how easy it is to calculate the differential or spread between the two groups of cards, let's go back to the example of a 20-card deal cited above. In that deal there were seven high cards and one 8. The 8 is neutral and not counted as part of either group; so you subtract one from 20, leaving 19. Since there were only seven high cards out of 19 total, there must have been 12 low cards. The resulting count of plus 5 is then carried forward to the next deal. Suppose on the next deal 18 cards were dealt, of which two were 8s and nine were high cards. We deduct the 2 from 18, leaving 16, and we know that the count on that deal was minus 2. There had to be seven low cards (16 minus 9). But we had carried a count of plus 5 into that deal, so our count now becomes plus 3.

In most single-deck games when 38 cards have been dealt, as in the examples just cited, there would be a new shuffle. However, some clubs still do deal to the end. Let's assume this is one of them and see what our plus 3 count tells us with only 14 cards left to deal. Since we've already seen three 8s, we know that those 14 cards must consist of one 8 and 13 other cards, eight of which are high and five low — still a very favorable mix for the player, and worth a maximum bet.

The significance of any plus or minus count increases as the cards are dealt and the number of cards remaining to be dealt grows smaller and smaller. If the above example had been a

TABLE 18
Bet-sizing Strategy Based on the "Count" (standard bet: 2 units)

| Cards dealt | Bet (units): | | | | | |
	1	2	3	4	5	6
Single-deck game						
10 – 15	at −4	−3 to +2	+3	+4	+5	+6 or more
20 – 30	−3	−2 to +2	+3	+3	+4	+5 or more
30 – 35	−2	−2 to +1	+2	+3	+3	+4 or more
Double-deck game						
10 – 15	at −6	−5 to +4	+5	+6	+7	+8 or more
20 – 30	−5	−4 to +3	+4	+5	+6	+8 or more
30 – 35	−5	−4 to +3	+4	+5	+6	+7 or more
40 – 50	−4	−3 to +2	+3	+4	+5	+7 or more
50+	same as single deck after 52 cards dealt.					
Four-deck game						
20 – 40	at −8	−7 to +6	+7	+8	+10	+12 or more
40 – 60	−7	−6 to +6	+7		+8	+10 or more
60 – 80	−7	−6 to +5	+6	+7	+8	+9 or more
80 – 100	−6	−5 to +5	+6		+7	+9 or more
100+	same as double-deck after 104 cards dealt.					

four-deck game, the plus 5 count on the first deal of 20 cards would have been next to meaningless. In terms of the 188 cards remaining, the plurality of five high cards would give the player a slight edge, but not enough to justify anything more than a very modest increase in the size of his bet.

You now know what I believe is the world's best and simplest method of judging the favorability of the conditions under which your next bet will be made. Your estimate of that degree of favorability or its lack, should always be a controlling factor in your betting strategy. You know, of course, that you're bound to lose many bets when the percentages are on your side and win many when they're not. But you can be confident that if you play those percentages consistently, you will be a

TABLE 19
Weighted Schedule for Taking or Refusing Insurance
(standard bet: 2 units)

Bet (units)	Take insurance
1	never
2	seldom
3	if you have 19 to 21, or 11
4	usually
5 or more	almost always

winner on balance — provided the games are run honestly.

The information given you by the differential count should not only influence the size of your bets, it should also alter your basic strategy for standing, hitting, doubling, splitting, and taking insurance. It would be virtually impossible to devise an explicit strategy for each of the thousands of card and count combinations that can occur in this game. Rigid betting schedules and strategy rules are therefore inappropriate.

Accordingly, the procedures and recommendations in the following paragraphs and Tables 18 through 22 are offered as guidelines rather than as advice which must always be strictly adhered to. Assume, if you will, that your standard bet with a fresh deck is two units. Now, as the "count" or differential ebbs and flows, you should, and I hope you will, raise and lower the size of your bets. I suggest that you do so about as indicated in Table 18.

Using Tables 18 through 22 as guides, when your indicated bet is two or three units, you will generally adhere to basic strategy for standing, doubling, splitting, and declining insurance. When your indicated bet is three or four units, insurance at 2 to 1 is apt to be a fair bet and should be taken if you have a really good hand such as 19 or 20, or possibly 11. With higher counts it should almost always be taken, and with a minus count, it should never be taken.

You may question the reliability of the hi-lo count as an indicator of the action to be taken when insurance is offered.

TABLE 20
Adjusted Strategy for Standing Based on the "Count" (standard bet: 2 units)

| Bet (units) | Dealer's up-card: | | | | | | | | | | Comments |
	A	10	9	8	7	6	5	4	3	2	
Hard hands											
1	17	17	17	17	17	12	13	13	13	14	
2 – 3	17	17*	17*	17	16	12	12	12	12	13	*see surrender option
4	16	15*	16*	16	16	12	12	12	12	12	
5 or more	15	14**	15	15*	15	12	12	12	12	12	**13 if deck very rich
Soft hands											
1	18	18	18	18	18	18	18	18	18	18	
2 – 3	18	19	19	18	18	19	19	19	19	18	
4	18	19	19	18	18	20	20	20	19	19	
5 or more	18	18	18	18	18	20	20	20	19	19	
Surrender (if allowed)											
3 or more	with hard 15 – 16 vs. dealer's 9 or 10										
4 or more	with hard 14 – 16 vs. dealer's 9 or 10										
5 or more	with hard 14 – 16 vs. dealer's 8, 9, 10										

TABLE 21
Adjusted Strategy for Doubling Based on the "Count" (standard bet: 2 units)

| Bet (units) | Dealer's up-card: | | | | | | | | | | Comments |
	A	10	9	8	7	6	5	4	3	2	
Hard hands											
1	11*	11*	11*	10*	10*	10	10	10	10*	10*	*If deck very poor,
2 – 3	10	11	11	10	10	8	9	9	9	9	don't double
4	10	11	10	10	9	8	8	8	8	9	
5 or more	10	11	10	9	9	8	8	8	8	9	

Soft hands

| Bet (units) | Dealer's up-card: | | | Comments |
	7	4 to 6	2 to 3	
1	A6*	A2 – A6	A2 – A6*	*No double if deck very poor
2 – 3		A2 – A7	A6 – A7**	**Double on soft 18 only if "count" is plus
4		A2 – A8	A6 – A7	
5 or more		A2 – A8	A6 – A7	

TABLE 22
Pair Splitting Strategy Based on the "Count"
(Split unless otherwise indicated)

Player's pair		1	2 – 3	4	5	Bet (units):
As	vs.	all	all	all	all	
10s	vs.	no	no	no*	no**	*can be split vs. 5, 6 **can be split vs. 4, 5, 6
9s	vs.	3 – 6	2 – 6, 8, 9	2 – 6, 8, 9	2 – 6, 8, 9	
8s	vs.	all	all	2 – 8*	2 – 8*	*surrender vs. 9, 10; or draw
7s	vs.	2 – 8	2 – 8	2 – 7*	2 – 7*	*surrender vs. 8 – 10; or draw
6s	vs.	2 – 7	2 – 7	2 – 6	2 – 6	
5s	vs.	no	no	no	no	
4s	vs.	2 – 6	no	no	no	
3s	vs.	2 – 7	2 – 7	2 – 6	2 – 6	
2s	vs.	2 – 7	2 – 7	2 – 6	2 – 6	

Since one-third of the high group are 9s and aces, a big plus count could mean that the deck was rich in those cards rather than 10s and face cards. I have found, however, that as one becomes accustomed to counting this way, he can't help observing any unusual distribution of the cards he's counting. If nearly all those cards have been 10-count, he will know that the remaining deck is poorer in these cards than his hi-lo count indicates — and vice-versa. So he will be guided accordingly. If he hasn't noticed any unusual ratio of 10s to 9s and aces, the strong probability is that his differential count is just about as accurate a measure of 10s as those systems which count 10s exclusively. And it is, of course, a much more accurate measure of the overall favorability of the deck than any 10-count system.

Table 19, on page 183, shows the weighted schedule for taking or refusing "insurance." The other refinements of basic strategy made possible by keeping close tabs on the condition of the deck are incorporated into Tables 20, 21, and 22.

CHAPTER 15

Choosing Your Casino

Or, Why Expert Blackjack Players Sometimes Lose

I commented earlier that over a period of years I had been a "fairly" successful 21 player. The word "fairly" seemed appropriate because for the last several years, while I've played quite frequently, my playing has generally been limited to short interludes away from the crap table — and my results have been spotty. Before that, blackjack had always been my favorite casino game and I had been a consistent winner for many years. I think it safe to say that I won 80 percent of the time.

Some time in the '60s, counting systems had begun to proliferate and to be widely promoted, so the casinos felt it necessary to protect themselves against a growing army of really skillful players. They instituted all kinds of countermeasures, some honest, some dishonest, and many in a sort of gray area — unfair perhaps, but not out-and-out cheating. Caution and selectivity became the order of the day for players who enjoyed the game too much to quit, but who did not enjoy being fleeced.

At some casinos, dealers were burying one or more cards after each deal. At others, dealers were concealing cards that should have been exposed. If a dealer had a blackjack, he might scoop up the players' cards face down; when a player busted, his hole cards would not be turned over; if the dealer did not have to play out his own hand, he would fail to expose his own hole card.

Reshuffling in the middle of the deck(s) or whenever a $5 bettor jumped his bet to $25 or so, became commonplace. Some dealers "counted" the deck right along with the customers, and whenever it became rich in high cards, that would be their signal to reshuffle. Along with these marginal countermeasures came the introduction of more and more multiple-deck games and the elimination of many single-deck tables. Single decks are a great deal easier to count than the others. At the major hotels on the Las Vegas Strip, almost all betting minimums were raised for the single-deck games, a move aimed directly at the small bettor whose counting system might call for some bets four or five times the size of his normal bet.

Of course, there had always been the sleight of hand artists, the so-called "mechanics" who could "stack" the deck, deal "seconds" or from either the top or bottom of the deck hidden in their hands. These dealers were sometimes held in "ready reserve" to be called into action whenever some customer was winning too consistently.

STACKING THE DECK

But I believe the principal form of cheating by dealers, then and now, comes under the general heading of stacking the deck. When my own results began to worsen, I noticed that the proportion of "stiffs" (hands with counts of 12 to 16) being dealt me seemed strangely large. Those hands normally account for about 41 percent of all possible two-card combinations, whereas the ratio for me seemed nearer to 60 percent or 70 percent.

One day two years ago I flew home from Las Vegas seated next to a young lady in her late 20s or early 30s. She was a school teacher about to change her profession to become a 21 dealer. Her new job at one of the major Strip hotels had been prearranged, and she had just finished her training at dealers' school. I inquired about that training and a shortened but accurate version of her reply follows. "The first week was devoted to teaching us the fundamentals and how to spot customer cheating. The next five weeks were devoted to teaching us how to cheat the customers."

Cheating instruction, she said, concentrated on the process known as "stripping" the deck. After a conventional shuffle, you may have noticed that most dealers slide clusters of cards back and forth through the deck in a way that looks natural enough but when you think about it, you realize that you've never seen that done in a private club or in a card game at a friend's home. That added touch following the shuffle is called "stripping," and my informant stated that the sole purpose of stripping by the 21 dealer is to improve your chances of starting out with a stiff. She said that the "students" were also taught special ways of picking up the cards during and after each deal, and they were advised that if they learned their lessons well, you, the customer, would probably get 10 percent to 25 percent more "stiffs" than you would otherwise.

I'm sure I don't have to tell you that no amount of expertise could possibly overcome the handicap of 10 percent to 25 percent extra "stiffs." So be on guard and alert; watch the dealer carefully and leave his or her table at the slightest indication of anything irregular — including an abnormal number of stiffs at your table for 10 or 15 consecutive deals. I'll touch on other things to look for, and dealers to avoid a bit later on, but now let's briefly consider some of the differences between casinos, as well as dealers.

HOUSE RULES

I mentioned earlier that Nevada rules for blackjack are quite liberal, but that they differ from club to club. Facilities and procedures also differ, sometimes markedly. When a place is unfamiliar it can be helpful to know the areas of possible differences, and also to have a basis for comparing the playing conditions at the various casinos. Table 23 includes most, if not all, of the procedural and rule divergences that you are likely to meet in Tahoe, Reno, and/or Las Vegas. The scoring that I've used is arbitrary, and you can substitute your own figures if you disagree with mine. Whatever figures you decide to use, they can be tallied to provide an excellent yardstick by which to measure the relative desirability of the various casinos you patronize.

A perfect score with the following schedule would be 90 or 91.

TABLE 23
A Blackjack Player's Scorecard for Evaluating Casinos

House rules	Score
Double down: on anything	10
Double down: on 10 and 11 only	0
Double down allowed on split hands	3
Pair splitting: any pair	7
Pair splitting: aces and 8s only	0
Additional splitting of split hands	3
Dealers stand on 17	10
Dealers must hit soft 17	7
Insurance pays 2 to 1	5
Blackjacks: pay 1½ to 1	10
Five cards under 22 pay 1½ to 1	3
Surrender privilege	5
Dealer wins ties	−100

Procedures and facilities	Score
15 tables or more	3
5 tables or less	0
Single-deck games	10
Double-deck games	5
Only four-deck games (shoes) players' cards exposed	2
Only four-deck games (shoes) cards dealt face down	0
Atmosphere: pleasant	5
Atmosphere: extra fast dealing	−5
Re-shuffles at end of deck(s)	5
Re-shuffles: after three-quarters of deck(s)	1
Re-shuffles: at dealer's whim	−5
Concealing cards: none	8
Concealing cards: few	2
Concealing cards: many	−10
Burying cards: 1 only	3
Burying cards: more	1
Maximum bet: at least 250 times minimum bet	1

I personally would not settle for a score of less than 52. The absolute essentials for me, reading down the list, would be these:

1. If nothing but four-deck games were available, the cards would have to be dealt face up.

2. The atmosphere would have to be pleasant and unhurried.

3. Reshuffles would be based on nothing but the number of cards left in the deck.

4. I consider concealing cards akin to cheating; I might accept it occasionally when it seemed accidental, but not often.

5. The right to double down on anything a "must."

6. The privilege of splitting any pair another "must."

7. Dealers must be required to hit any 16 and stand on any 17 except possibly a "soft" 17.

8. When the dealer has an ace up, the insurance bet at 2 to 1 odds is another "must."

9. Blackjacks must pay 1½ to 1 for the players, but not for the dealer.

10. If you ever stumble into a place where the dealer wins all ties, run — don't walk — to the nearest exit.

CHEATING AT BLACKJACK

A friend called the other day to ask if I'd seen a recently published article in which blackjack was extolled as the only casino game in which the players had a real chance to win. My response was negative on all counts. I had not seen the article and I consider the chance of winning at craps at least as good, if not better, than at 21. I added, of course, that I would agree with the author of that article if 21 dealers and games were uniformly honest and if the games were conducted fairly under the rules generally prevailing in Nevada.

The ingenuous public has been led to believe that honesty of the games is guaranteed by the twin facts of state control and the existence of an instrument of the state known as the Nevada Gaming Control Board. This body is supposed to have its agents gumshoeing around in all the casinos, on the lookout for any and all irregularities — and ready at the drop of a hat to close down the "joint" or do whatever else needs doing in order to protect the customers. The typical rejoinder to anyone voicing suspicions of cheating is that the idea is preposterous — too absurd to consider. . . . How could a huge and obviously prosperous enterprise risk being closed down for the sake of a few hundred or a few thousand dollars?

Now let's look at some of the practical aspects of the matter. The state of Nevada derives the lion's share of all of its tax revenues directly and indirectly from its gambling operations. An aura of respectability for those operations is essential if Vegas, Reno, and Tahoe are to continue to attract millions of visitors and thousands of conventions, as they do each year. So the state, in its own interest, provides that aura, while its primary concern is obviously the end result of all those visitors and conventions; namely those tax revenues and the prosperity of the state as a whole. Politicians are notoriously sensitive to which side of the bread their butter is on — and Nevada, like the other 49 states, is run by politicians.

Expert cheating is extremely difficult to detect or prove, even at the moment it takes place. It is almost always impossible to prove after the fact. Thus, in a dispute between an irate customer and a major hotel-casino employing some 10,000 people, the customer will be portrayed as a sore loser, and one can be fairly confident that that position will be upheld by the Gaming Control Board. The only sensible action for the average player who has been cheated or treated unfairly is to avoid that dealer or that casino thenceforth.

Many respected writers on this subject, including Thorp, Wilson, Scarne, and Roberts, go to great lengths to describe the modus operandi of card sharks and card "mechanics." They all agree that cheating is widespread even in the big-name Nevada casinos — and that it is far easier to cheat in card games than in any of the other games of chance. My own assumption is that you readers are not nearly so much concerned with how the cheaters do it, as you are with how you personally can protect yourself. My suggestions on that score follow.

Be aware that unless the cheater is quite clumsy you are unlikely to catch him in the act. Even if you did, it would be your word against his, and the management personnel to whom you might complain could hardly be expected to be impartial. In general, you are going to have to rely upon the combination of your own intuition and close observation. Be concerned:

1. If the dealer almost hides the deck in his hand and moves the hand around so that you can scarcely tell the top of the deck from the bottom; he may be "reversing" the deck — dealing from either end.

2. If he holds the cards so high that the player can't see that he's dealing the top card in the deck.

3. If his eyes seem to be fixed on the deck rather than on the player to whom he's dealing.

4. If at any point during the deal the hand holding the cards is hidden from view by his other hand.

5. If he appears to pick up the players' cards in any methodical way other than the exact order in which they were dealt.

6. If he almost invariably draws a 10-count card for himself when it would be advantageous — or a low card when a high card would put him over 21.

7. If he seems to take great pains with his shuffling and "stripping" procedure.

8. If, as mentioned above, you and the other players are persistently dealt an abnormally high percentage of "stiffs" — well over 50 percent.

When you are concerned, the thing to do is to leave. Aside from these indications of possible skullduggery, other excellent causes for concern would be concealment of cards, reshuffling whenever the deck was favorable, and very fast dealing and hand movements.

In his book *The Casino Gambler's Guide*, Alan Wilson has a chapter entitled "Will They Let You Win?" In that chapter he tells of one of David Susskind's "Open End" programs broadcast over nationwide television, in which cheating at cards in Nevada casinos was thoroughly aired by Dr. Edward Thorp, author of *Beat the Dealer*, and Michael MacDougall, a prominent magician and card manipulator. One of the participants in that program was Harold Smith, Jr., son of the manager of Harolds Club in Reno. Wilson commented that Smith made no attempt to defend the casinos or to deny the allegations of cheating made by the other panel members.

My guess is that 90 percent or more of the Nevada blackjack games are honest in the strictest sense of that word, but that in 90 percent of the "honest" games nearly unbeatable countermeasures are routinely employed against skillful players whose winnings pose any kind of threat to a club's bankroll. These "honest" games are more often than not "off limits" to known expert players. Being barred by most of the well-known casinos is the ultimate testimony to one's skill (when it doesn't happen for some reason other than skill) — and the list of those so honored is quite long.

SUMMARY

From all of the foregoing you will have correctly surmised that to consistently win worthwhile sums at Nevada blackjack is no simple matter. Skill coupled with patience and extreme alertness is absolutely essential. My own recipe for success might be summarized as follows:

1. Study and learn basic strategy until it becomes second nature. Once you have it down pat, horse sense will guide you when the deck is either rich or poor, whether or not you've memorized the recommended strategy for each situation in those circumstances.

2. Practice card counting at home, dealing more and more rapidly as it becomes easier for you. Whether you use the Hi-Lo Differential system or some other system, it is essential for you to know the general character of the undealt cards if you expect to have an edge over the house. Whatever system you use, if you should find it too difficult to keep running counts of the high cards or the 10s as well as the total number of cards dealt, forget the latter.

You will be able to estimate how many cards have been dealt at any given time.

3. If your regular bet is $1 or $2, your maximum can be $5 or $10, but ordinarily your big bet should not be such as to attract undue attention, which means not more than three times your regular bet. Your regular bet should never be more than 4 percent of your stake. That limitation could still call for a bet equivalent of 24 percent of your bankroll whenever you doubled down or split pairs after a maximum bet.

4. If you expect to wager as much as $20 on a hand, play in the large plush casinos — and preferably at tables where others are betting as much or more than you are.

5. Be nonchalant in your manner, and if possible, look and act like a loser. If you do not like your dealer and feel inclined to say something that might antagonize him, don't. Leave the table instead. If you are about to leave a table a winner, make a good bet for the dealer and then leave, win, lose, or draw.

6. Re-read the score sheet for casinos in this chapter and my comments thereon, and be guided accordingly. Watch the dealer's hands and the cards carefully — and if you have any doubts as to the honesty or the basic fairness of the game — leave the table.

7. Make it a habit never to allow yourself to lose more than 20 percent of your stake at one table.

8. If possible, select a seat toward the left (third base) side of the table. This will enable you to see a maximum number of cards before you have to make your decision regarding standing, hitting, doubling, or splitting.

9. Until you are very expert and very fast at counting, avoid head-to-head games or tables with only one other player. Counting when there are less than three players is far more difficult than at a full or nearly full table.

CHAPTER 17

Wrapping It Up

My comments on various gambling techniques and systems have frequently included (but not defined) the phrase "rapid escalation." For systems in which losses are recovered via increased bets, the rate of needed increase is predetermined by the amount of prior loss, thus posing no real problem. However, for systems calling for escalated winning bets, it is not easy to calculate the rate of escalation most likely to yield optimum results.

Many old-time gamblers favor escalating by drawing down just half of each winning bet after the second win in a series. I would call that "fast escalation." The arithmetic of various ways of scaling up one's winning bets may help you decide how you would like to do it (see Table 24, page 198). My own reaction to the three rates of escalation compared in that table is as follows:

> FAST: *Excellent —* if you stop on a winning bet or after just one loss.
>
> SLOW: *Poor —* Rate of gain too slow; only advantage applies to small wagers that won't materially affect one's fortunes.
>
> MEDIUM: *Excellent —* equals the "Fast" progression for the first six wins, and can take two losses at the upper end of the series without going into the minus column.

When betting on an even or nearly-even proposition, the likelihood of eight or more consecutive right guesses is very slim — 1 in 256 tries — and there is always a chance of two consecutive losses in the middle of a good run. When serious money is at stake, I like a system that can comfortably weather a couple of losses; hence my preference for the above "me-

TABLE 24

End Results of Escalating Winning Bets at Differing Rates

Bet series	Cumulative profit	Net profit if bet lost
Fast rate		
5		
10	15	(5)
15	30	0
23	53	7
35	88	18
53	141	35
80	221	61
120	341	101
180	521	161
Medium rate		
5		
10	15	(5)
15	30	0
25	55	5
35	90	20
45	135	45
55	190	80
65	255	125
75	330	180
Slow rate		
5		
6	11	(1)
7	18	4
8	26	10
9	35	17
10	45	25
11	56	34
12	68	44
13	81	55

dium" rate of bet escalation as opposed to either the "fast" or "slow" rate.

The system you are about to learn is by long odds the most dramatically effective one I know — and the rate at which it requires winning bets to be escalated is what I have termed "medium."

THE BARSTOW SYSTEM

You may recall the first paragraph of the introduction to this book, in which I stated that between any two opposing even chances, one was likely to be dominant at any given time. Repeat sequences of such chances will account for roughly 50 percent of all decisions. I stated that there were betting procedures that could capitalize on this obvious fact. The Barstow System is one — and it is the only system to which I have been willing to lend my own name. Hopefully, you will find it to be worth its weight in gold and/or coin of the realm.

This system is ideal for the low percentage games such as craps, baccarat, and single-zero roulette. It will probably hold its own against two zeros in roulette, but that has not been tested. Incidentally, when using it in craps and betting the pass line, I suggest that you do *not* take odds unless you are beyond the third number in your bet progression. Actually, it is questionable whether you should take odds at any stage.

Barstow's basic strategy is not especially complicated. You use one of the following bet series:

A. 1 2 3 5 7 9 11 — preferred

B. 1 2 4 6 8 10 12 — aggressive

C. 1 2 3 5 8 11 14 — aggressive

D. 1 2 4 7 10 13 16 — more aggressive

The numbers represent your betting units, which may be $1 $2 $5 $10 or $25 each. Starting with the smallest bet, you move up the series as you win. When you lose a bet, your next bet is lowered by one unit. If the spacing between bets at the point where you lose (beyond the second or third number in your bet series) happens to be $4 or four units or more, you would drop back half the distance to the next lower number in your series after the loss. When you win one or more bets after a loss, you escalate at the same rate called for by your bet series at that point. (In series "A" above, if you lost the 5 and then won your next three bets, they would be 4, 6, and 8; in series "C" they would be 4, 7, and 10.)

1. The first bet in any new series is optional and not too important. If the preceding series had ended with a sequence of three or more repeat decisions, I'd usually start a new series betting the other way.

2. When you lose a one-unit bet, your next bet is one unit the other way, *i.e.*, the reverse of your preceding bet. If you lose on pass, bet don't pass. If you lose two consecutive one-unit bets, skip the next decision, and when you resume, bet that the skipped decision will repeat. (Skipping reduces the number of losses that might be caused by a long sequence of alternating decisions.)

3. Generally, you will end any series and start a new one whenever:
   a. You've won the first three bets, the first four out of five, or five out of seven including the last three.
   b. Profit on a series is more than 6 units.
   c. Loss on a single series reaches 30 units.
   d. When you've had three (five at most) more winning bets than losers in a single series.
   e. When you've lost three successive bets totaling 15 or more units.

4. If you've won your last two bets totaling 10 units or more, and have a small profit (less than 6 units) or a small loss (less than 4 units), you *may* end the series. If you elect to continue it, your next bet should be one or two units smaller than the last winning bet. In the same circumstance, if you still have a loss exceeding 3 units, continue the series dropping back at least one unit for the next bet. This kind of back-pedalling should be done only *once* in any single series.

5. If loss on a series reaches 20 units, pull back (*one time only*) to the second or third number in your bet series.

6. Never try to go beyond the seventh number in your bet series. This holds regardless of your profit or loss position, or the size of your bankroll. If you want to accelerate your winnings, best procedure is to increase the size of your betting units; next best would be to switch from Series "A" to Series "B," "C," or "D".

7. When there has been a sequence of 5 successive repeat decisions, or 6 out of 7 including the last two decisions, bet the sequence will end. If this should result in two consecutive losses, do as follows:

   a. At the one-unit level, reverse again and go with the trend.

   b. Above the four-unit level, end the series.

   c. At any other level, either end the series, stop betting temporarily, or change tables.

This trend-reversal procedure has proven so rewarding, that I've frequently used it even when that meant ignoring some of the disciplines previously mentioned.

If you segregate chips representing 20 units at the start of each new bet series, you will always be able to keep fairly close tabs on your profit and loss position.

Probably the best advice I can offer is: (1) When in doubt, end the series; and (2) try always to end each series with one or more winning bets. When you *begin* a new series, the system tends to force you to "swim with the tide." If you prolong a series in which your bets are beyond the third number, you can find yourself "swimming against the tide." It is good policy, therefore, to accept short profits as well as shorter losses.

Of course, when a series starts off with a lot of one and two-unit losses, you will be unable to keep it as short as you'd like, but when the turn comes, as it nearly always does, each win can offset three or four losers. Some of my most profitable series have begun with a half-dozen or more small losses.

If you plan to bet with $5 units, a bankroll of $350 should prove adequate. You should win at least twice for each time you lose in a typical four-hour session. My own record is considerably better than that. At this writing I've demonstrated the system to 12 individuals. Each demonstration covered about 240 dice decisions — roughly four hours at the tables — betting in $5 increments with a $350 stake. In 10 instances profits averaged over $300, while in the two losing trials the losses were $80 and $100, respectively. My biggest loss at any point was just under $350.

One of the aforementioned successful demonstrations appeared at the start to be headed for certain failure. We were at the MGM Grand in Las Vegas and I had bet my companion that the system would win at least $200 in 240 decisions at the crap tables. She recorded each bet I made and I was limited to a maximum bet of $50. The time involved was slightly more than four hours. The record of all bets made in that test may prove instructive, so I have compiled it in tabular form and in units of $5 each. Refer to Table 25.

Note that if I had ended the first series above after winning my first three bets, as I probably should have, my score would have been plus six instead of minus two units. Note also that there were eight instances when after winning $25 or more, I backtracked to a small bet instead of continuing to escalate. In the miserable third series I lost 13 of my first 16 bets; and later in the same series, when the system called for maximum bets of 10 units, I lost that top bet three times. Yet, despite all that grief, I was able to end the series with a net loss of only two units.

Note also that each of the series ended with a sequence of winning bets, the poorest of which was three out of four. You may have observed that near the middle of the demonstration I changed my up progression from 1-2-3 to 1-2-4. There is no rigid rule as to how fast one escalates; if he wishes to play aggressively, he will widen the spacing between his winning bets — and vice versa if he wishes to play conservatively.

TABLE 25

The Barstow System in Action (247 bets at the MGM Grand Hotel, Las Vegas)

Series no.	Profit or loss on each bet ($5 units)	Profit (loss)
1	1 2 3 (5) 4 (6) (5) (4) 3 (5) 4 6	(2)
2	1 (2) 1 (2) (1) (1) 0 (1) 1 2 (3) (2) 1 (2) (1) 1 (2) (1) 1 (2) (1) 1 (2) (1) 1 2 (3) 2 (4) (3) 2 4 (6) (5) (4) 3 5 7 3 (5) 4 6	(6)
3	(1) (1) 0 (1) (1) 0 (1) 1 (2) (1) (1) 0 1 (2) (1) 1 (2) (1) (1) 0 1 2 3 (5) 4 (6) 5 (7) 6 8 (10) (9) 8 (10) 9 (10) 9 (5) 4 6 8	(2)
4	1 (2) (1) 1 (2) (1) (1) 0 (1) (1) 0 1 2 3 (5) (4) (3) (2) (1) (1) 0 1 (2) 1 (2) 1 (2) 1 (2) (1) 1 (2) (1) 0 1 2 4 6 (3) 2 4 (6) 5 (7) 6 (8) 7 (9) 8 (10) 3 5 7 9	2
5	1 2 (4) (3) 2 4 6 (8) 7 3	10
6	(1) 1 (2) 1 (1) (1) 0 (1) 1 2 (4) 3 5	3
7	(1) (1) 0 (1) (1) 0 (1) 1 2 (4) 3 5	2
8	(1) (1) 0 (1) 1 (2) 1 2 (4) (3) 2 4 6	4
9	(1) (1) 0 (1) 1 2 (4) 3 5 7	11
10	1 2 (4) 3 (5) 4 (6) 5 3 5	8
11	1 (2) 1 2 (4) 3 5	6
12	(1) (1) 0 1 2 (4) 3 (5) (4) 3 (5) 4 6 (3) 2 4 (5) (4) (3) (2) 1 2 (4) 3 5 7	2
13	1 (2) 1 2 4	6
14	(1) (1) 0 1 2 4 6 3	14

Cumulative net: 58 units or $290.00

"Choppy" Dice — An Alternative Procedure

When the dice or the wheel or the cards are "choppy" — few repeat sequences and few periods of dominance by one side or the other — the foregoing procedure can prove frustrating. In that case my first recommendation is to change tables, especially if one nearby appears to be very "hot" or very "cold." My second suggestion is to alter your basic bet-selection procedure as follows:

Use your same bet series and bet any way you like on the first two decisions. From then on bet that each new decision will alternate from being the *same* as the second preceding decision, to being the *opposite* of the second preceding decision. For example, if the pattern of the last few decisions had been + + −, your next bet might be plus (same as second preceding). If you won that bet, the pattern would then be + + − + and your next bet would still be plus since that would be the opposite of the second preceding decision. When you lose any bet, you continue betting either *opposite to*, or the *same as* the second preceding decision, whichever way you were betting when you lost. When you win, you resume alternating.

You'll always know what the second preceding decision was if you will rack or stack your chips of two different denominations, in the same pattern as the last four or five decisions.

These procedures may not be the final answer to obtaining optimum results, but they've proven quite effective for me. With minimum deviation, betting $5 units with a stake of $350, my results in 18 Nevada sessions averaging two and one-half hours each, have been as follows:

Won 14 times with an average profit per session of $243.
Lost 4 times with an average loss per session of $129.

The effectiveness of this system is attributable mainly to three factors:

1. It seems to give one a slightly better than even chance of betting the side that will dominate in the short run.
2. Sequences of winning bets must occur from time to time, and when they do, a few such at the end of a series usually offset a great many losing bets that may have preceded them.
3. THE 4 BASIC DISTRIBUTION PATTERNS (up 2 units; down 1 unit)

+20	+30	+40	+50.......+140	Win-loss ratio
−20	−15	−10	− 5 ....(50)	14:8
+20	−30	+25	−35 ....(20)	(Ratio decreases as
−20	+15	−25	+20 ....(10)	numbers get bigger)

There's an old saying in Wall Street that goes, "Trees don't grow to heaven." I suggest that you keep it in mind whenever you're having a nice little run of winning bets.

DISCIPLINE

You have tested a variety of systems against the record of many thousands of casino decisions and, after much trial and error experimenting, you've found two or three procedures that really do well. They win more often than not, or when they win, the profits more than offset prior losses. Congratulations seem to be in order. You've got it made — or have you?

No, my friend, you haven't got it made, not yet. Your real battle lies ahead. When you're locked in a contest with a casino, the toughest battle you face is with yourself. If you've done your homework, you know what you should do, but doing it is quite another matter.

In a casino one is subject to all kinds of extraneous influences; not only that, he is dealing with hard cash instead of numbers on a piece of paper. Every few minutes there will be what seems a valid reason for minor or major modification of the system he worked out so carefully and painstakingly. One can't eliminate those subconscious urges, or the feeling that if it worked on paper, it ought to do doubly well when you can see who's throwing the dice, or when you have the benefit of knowing the numbers or colors or cards that came up just prior to the last decision.

After all, those tabulations on paper only tell you what happened; they can't tell you what caused the happening, whether the shooter was a man or a woman, lucky or unlucky, or if one of the dice had just bounced off the table. In a casino you're dealing with reality, with flesh-and-blood people.

Certainly the things you can see and feel should enter into your calculations — but to what extent should they govern your actions? My answer to this question is an unequivocal negative. If your system really does well on paper, it should work in the casino — and the less you tamper with it, the greater the likelihood that it will perform as expected.

Discipline is a prime requisite for success in any undertaking. It is every bit as essential in gambling games as it would be if one were starting a new business. As a matter of fact, you may find it helpful to think of each of your visits to a casino as a brand new business venture — and to resolve that if it fails, it won't be for want of all the skill, intelligence, and discipline that you can bring to it.

More on "Foolproof Systems"

Gambling is a subject upon which one might expound and expand interminably. This doubtless reflects the mystery of why it should be so difficult to devise an unbeatable — and practical — system for winning in an even or nearly even game of chance. The real problem relates more to practicality than to certainty.

We have already seen that the simplest of all systems for betting on even chances — raising one's bets one unit at a time, win or lose, will virtually guarantee a net profit at some point. That system, however, is woefully impractical.

A different and equally simple procedure would also virtually insure a profit without as much risk of requiring several hundred bets, and perhaps reaching the house limit before the profit was achieved. This would be to raise one's bets $2 or two units after each win, and to lower them $1 or one unit after each loss. Doing this, one would almost never have to wager as much as $50 or 50 units before he had his profit.

It seems to me that the most reliable prescription for a nearly foolproof system would be to take any good system that wins at least as often as it loses, and has a profit potential larger than its loss potential, and use it in the following way:

First: Strictly limit loss in a single session to an easily affordable amount — and regard that amount as your "stake."

Second: Your profit objective in most 4 or 5 hour sessions should be at least two or three times the maximum loss you are willing to accept.*

---

*Not applicable if one uses a system such as "Fibonacci" in which risk of *any* loss in 4 or 5 hours would be minute and rate of gain correspondingly slow.

Third: Increase the size of your bets by 50 percent *or more* whenever your stake or bankroll has been doubled — and by another 50 percent when it has been tripled. With each increase in your unit size, your loss limit should also be changed; viz: From the point at which your stake has been doubled any subsequent loss should be held to a figure that would insure your doing no worse than breaking even for the session. If you triple your original stake, any subsequent loss should be limited to an amount that leaves you with not less than 200 percent of your original stake.

Fourth: Whenever in any session your *profit* reaches three or more times the amount of your original stake, either stop at that point or limit any subsequent loss to no more than 10 or 15 percent of your maximum bankroll from then on.

In the above context, the "Barstow System" would appear to qualify as a likely candidate for "foolproof" honors.

THE PARTNERSHIP CONCEPT

Two players functioning as a team and betting progressively after either winning or losing bets, can both win even if they use the same system but bet on opposing even chances. This partnership concept has the important virtue of smoothing out peaks and valleys in each of the partner's results.

In earlier discussions of the advantages of team play in which two players using the same system bet oppositely, I may carelessly have indicated that the team would have to have two opposing bets on the table most of the time. That is not the case.

In craps if the shooter threw a 12 while one partner had $30 on don't pass and the other had $20 on pass, the team would lose $20 and gain nothing. On the other hand, if only the $10 difference between those two bets had been wagered on don't, there would have been no loss at all.

In roulette a team with two opposing bets on the table would pay a severe penalty whenever a zero came up. If their wagers had been $20 and $30, as in the preceding example, their loss would be $50, contrasted with just $10 if they had bet only the net difference.

Solution: one partner does the betting for both. The other partner with notebook in hand keeps track of the two opposing positions and figures the net difference between the next two bets their system calls for. He then tells his partner the single bet that reflects that difference.

Suppose the team is using the "2-5" system described on page 81. Their bet series might be 5 7 10 15 25. (Incidentally, this is an excellent series.) If partner A below wins the first two bets while partner B loses them, no money has changed hands and the scorekeeper's record looks like this:

	A	B	Net
	5	− 5	0
	7	− 7	0
next bet	5	10	5 — First partnership bet

Scorekeeper now says to his teammate, "B bets $5." This modus operandi is not too difficult to master, and it also has the great virtue of eliminating the likelihood of a less experienced partner failing to carry out his assignments properly. That partner, of course, would be the one who did the actual betting while the "captain" of the team kept score.

The advantages of partnership play are nicely illustrated by the story of two little old ladies playing roulette and using Labouchere or the Cancellation system at the Dunes Hotel in Las Vegas, as told by Major Riddle in his entertaining book *The Weekend Gambler's Handbook.* The ladies were sisters and one of them bet on red while the other bet on black. Each of the sisters, of course, was an odds-on favorite to win her own series — and in fact each of them did win for quite some time.

Riddle doesn't say exactly how many days the two sisters played before the system failed them, but he implies that they played for more than a week. Finally there came a point where the system called for one of the sisters to bet more than $200.

She made the bet and lost, whereupon she and her sister decided it was time to say goodbye to the Dunes Hotel.

There are two object lessons in that story. One, as I've tried to make clear, is that with a sensible bet system, two persons betting opposite to each other can both win. The other is that with any progression in which bets escalate as one loses, there must be a reasonable cut-off point. If the two ladies had played for a week, they must have won at least 500 Labouchere series before giving up. Riddle's concluding comment was, "They were probably the two wisest roulette players I have ever met," clearly suggesting that they quit good winners.

FAST ACTION SYSTEMS

For excitement and pure enjoyment coupled with the potential for big and fast profits, nothing, in my opinion, can touch those crap systems which permit players to capitalize on the long runs between 7s that occur quite often. "Pass Come Plus the Odds" is one of these (page 104). Another is "Pass plus the Numbers" (page 105). Others include the "Counteraction" systems (page 110) and the "Free Double Odds" system (page 107).

If you use any of these systems, I suggest that most of your bet escalating be done after you have a cushion of profits rather than while you're attempting to build that cushion.

ROULETTE AND THE "SCIENTIFIC" SYSTEM

If you are ever lucky (and persevering) enough to discover a biased wheel, you may be able to make a fortune at this game. But spotting such a wheel is much easier said than done. One would have to clock at least 3,800 spins to be reasonably sure, and then he'd have to have some reliable means of identifying the particular wheel in case its location was changed by the casino.

The job of finding such a wheel might require hundreds of hours, after which there would always be the risk of non-cooperation by the casino. If it suspected that anything was amiss, it would surely take the wheel out of play.

For some strange reason this approach to roulette has generally been labeled by writers on the subject as "scientific." In any event many stories have been told of fortunes being won with it, but be warned: even if you should find a couple of numbers or a segment of a wheel that deviated from the norm by as much as 20 percent, it would take a lot of capital and time to begin to repay you for your effort.

My basic prescription for double-zero roulette is simple and unhedged: minimize your risk. Play for parlays on the even chances. If you like to bet on "sleepers," limit yourself to low-budget progressions of no more than three bets on the even chances, five bets on the 2 to 1 propositions, and perhaps 10 to 15 bets on the 8 to 1 and 11 to 1 "finals." Generally I prefer progressions in which you escalate as you win, rather than as you lose; the Step Ladder or Barstow, for example. If Labouchere fascinates you, play it confining your bets to the even-money "sleepers" or use the "pattern" method of bet selection and plan to abandon any Labouchere series when your next bet would have to be more than five times the amount of the profit you're playing for, and drop the system entirely if losses with it accumulate to a point where they represent as much as 15 to 20 percent of your stake.

BLACKJACK AFTERTHOUGHTS

Originally I recommended limiting your maximum bets in this game to no more than three times your normal bet, the object being to avoid unwanted attention by the casino management. However, if you are anxious to maximize the rate at which you can win, you can parlay winning bets without attracting undue attention, provided that you do so more or less habitually. You should, of course, attempt a parlay only when the deck remains favorable after a win, or occasionally after a shuffle.

As a general rule, I would avoid any type of progressive betting in 21, but as I may have commented earlier, all rules have their exceptions. If you're playing in luck, you may feel that you can afford the risk of a short progression with a modest upward bias. But be careful; adverse runs in this game can be long and painful.

The above comments refer only to progressive raising of losing bets. Escalating winning bets is quite another matter, but the problem in blackjack is the constantly changing condition of the deck; its favorability or lack thereof for the player. However, on a recent visit to Las Vegas, I was agreeably surprised to find that the Barstow system, somewhat modified, could be used comfortably and effectively. Here's how I used it at a two-deck table:

My regular bet was $5, and when the deck was *neutral* or favorable, I used this progression: 5 6 8 12 16 20. Whenever the deck turned unfavorable I bet $5 no matter what my previous bet had been; then, when it became neutral or better, I resumed betting at the level in my series where I had last been scheduled to bet.

When I lost $8 or less, I dropped back $1; otherwise $2. My results in a two-hour session seemed at least as good, if not better, than they would have been had I simply raised and lowered my bets in accordance with the "count." Of course, the outcome in this isolated instance could have been due to luck on many of the deals when the deck was neutral.

One habit that can often prove rewarding is to always show your hole cards to your neighbors. They are likely to respond by showing you theirs, and that of course can be very helpful with your count. This practice may lead to distracting conversation by said neighbors. If so, you'll have the problem of weighing its pros and cons and proceding accordingly.

A final cautionary note: be very choosy about where you play — and be very quick to change tables or casinos whenever things don't seem to be quite as they should be.

Epilogue

In discussing these games and systems, I have tried to steer a middle course between excessive enthusiasm and excessive cynicism. Yet I suspect that my choice of words has not always reflected my true convictions and feelings as accurately as I might have wished. So in this final chapter I shall try to piece together a few "loose ends."

All of the systems described and recommended in preceding chapters give the player a "fair shake" and a fair chance to win, unless otherwise noted. These systems may not be the best that will ever be devised, but I believe they are as good or better than any that have been published up to now. I have tried to present them honestly and without extravagant and unsupported claims.

No doubt I've merely scratched the surface in this extraordinarily complex and fascinating field. Just as there is no end to the dreams men can dream, there will continue to be no end to sometimes ingenious and sometimes phony systems ostensibly designed to "beat the game" and extract money from the greedy casinos. Regrettably, many of these systems will have been fashioned primarily in order to separate the unwary and the naive from their money.

When you buy a book with a title like *Beat The Casino*, you expect its contents to be usable and worthwhile; that is, unless you happen to be a "dyed in the wool" cynic. In that case, you would know in advance that said contents would prove worthless. My hope, of course, is that you have found the title of this book not to be misleading.

I also hope that you will never lose sight of the fact that there is no way to eliminate the element of luck in any game in which chance plays a part. That applies to contract bridge as well as to all casino games. Lest this sound somewhat like a typical hedge clause, let me here restate my conviction that at least two of the partnership systems described in Chapter 6 and two or three of the other systems for individual play do, in fact, reverse the percentages and swing them over to the player's side — provided always that they are used properly. Yet I cannot promise that you'll win each time you use any one of these.

I might have chosen to call this work "The Royal Road to Riches," but I didn't. For the record, I want to make it clear that I do not suggest any casino game as a means of livelihood. On the other hand, I do recommend casinos and their games as far likelier sources of fun and profit than any other gambling media.

DIMINISHING PROBABILITY

As anything grows older, its life expectancy grows shorter. This is a basic law of nature and it makes no difference what the "thing" is. However, I know of no mathematics equation that confirms this natural (or physical) law. On the contrary, we are taught in school that when something has happened 10 times in succession, there is as much chance that it will repeat that performance and reach 20 consecutive as there was at the outset that it would do 10 consecutive.

I contend that when an even-money proposition has repeated 10 times, it no longer has its original 1 in 8 chance of repeating three more times. Maybe I could prove this if I understood Einstein's Theory of Relativity. As it is, I must rest my case on all the records of repeat occurrences that I've ever seen. Somewhere along the line they all show a much sharper drop-off in numbers than is prescribed by the laws of probability. (The actuarial tables that determine life insurance premiums are not based on pure mathematical formulae. They are based on mortality records and projections derived from those records; in a word, *experience*.)

More to the point, I've met a number of Nevada residents who admit to making their livings at the tables — and the two who were willing to confide their methods both did it "the hard way." They waited for what I have called "spot situations" and then jumped in.

The other day I had a phone call from a contractor who earns $40,000 or more per year but who can't stand losing at the tables. He proudly informed me that he had just returned from a Las Vegas weekend with a lady, and that he had covered expenses with $300 to spare. I promised not to tell exactly how he did it, so I can say only that he picked his "spots" at the crap tables with *extreme* care and used a five-stage Martingale. In the course of 25 or 30 hours at the tables — *without losing a single bet series* — he managed to win $500.

That kind of gambling isn't much fun, and I'm not recommending it. However, the point I'm trying to make should be clear. Mother Nature's *"Law of Action and Re-action"* will never be rescinded. Don't let anyone tell you that you can't improve your chances if you bide your time and pick your "spots."

USING THE DATA IN THIS BOOK

Most of you, I imagine, will pick one or two of what seem the most promising systems for your favorite game, and concentrate on them. Perhaps you'll practice at home — always a good idea — and then decide on one that seems to outperform the others and use it at your next opportunity.

My own suggestion would be that you pick at least three systems, and thoroughly familiarize yourself with them. One, of course, should have what looks like the best profit potential with the least risk. Another might be a good system for "choppy" tables. A third ought to be a "safe" and relaxing system, one that couldn't cost too much under the worst of circumstances. Other choices might be "the most action with maximum chance to make a killing," or "the most action with the smallest risk."

Whatever your taste and inclinations, you may as well

resign yourself to the fact that the pattern of decisions in all casino games is likely to be "choppy" more than half the time. That means "rough sledding" for systems that thrive on mathematical aberrations such as long runs of a single color, of passes, of alternating decisions, or numbers hit between 7s, etc.

Most systems in which winning bets are escalated do poorly in a "choppy" environment, while their opposite numbers are apt to perform nicely. So systems that need only one or two winning bets in order to produce a profit are well worth serious attention. Many of the progressions in Chapter 6 fit this category — and in this connection I'll remind you once again that familiarity with my pet bet-selection methods in Chapter 2 should prove beneficial.

Selecting those systems that best fit the five classifications mentioned above is not easy. What is best for me may not be for you. However, some of you may find my personal choices interesting or even instructive, so here they are:

Best All-around System

> BARSTOW, page 199

>> This one should do well in any environment, but it requires skillful handling. With $25 chips it can average $300 hourly profit.

"Choppy-table" Systems

> SUPER MARTINGALE, page 79

> FIBONACCI, page 75

>> Should be fairly safe using a 10-digit bet series.

> PARLAY PROGRESSIONS, page 66

>> Use with partner.

> 2 – 5 SYSTEM, page 81

> PLACING THE 6 AND 8, page 114

Systems for Relaxing

> ROULETTE PARLAYS, page 150

>> Use single even-money propositions.

REVERSE STEPLADDER, page 91
> Adjust progression to suit.

COLUMN AND DOZEN "SLEEPERS," page 148

BLACKJACK, page 164
> With very small standard bet.

To Make a "Killing"

PASS, COME, PLUS THE ODDS, page 104
> You may wish to use only two come bets until you're "in the money."

COUNTERACTION PROCEDURE No. 3, page 112

FREE DOUBLE ODDS, page 107

BLACKJACK, pages 210 and 211
> Possibly using the Barstow method of bet escalation in conjunction with the "count."

Most Action — Least Risk

TREADMILL, page 119
> Procedure number 1.

ROULETTE, page 135
> Play 10 numbers "straight up" with 10¢ chips.

COUNTERACTION PROCEDURE No. 1, page 111
> Use 25¢ chips.

I would call these selections "representative" rather than "exclusive." There are unquestionably many other systems in the book that fit the various categories as well, if not better than, those listed.

It is nice to hear about the guy who parlayed 15 consecutive right guesses at craps or baccarat, thereby increasing his net worth from $50 to $9,000 — or the V.I.P. who combined a bit of extrasensory perception with a shop-worn crap system that normally yields a 20 percent profit to the house and thus was able to "take" the Las Vegas establishment on each of 10 consecutive visits, for the tidy sum of $170,000.

Then there was the recent story in the press about a lady who was reported to have won $280,000 on a slot machine at the Las Vegas Hilton. Whether these stories are fact or fiction, we probably shall never know. We do, however, know two things: first, they make entertaining reading and are excellent "grist for the mill"; second, things like that are never going to happen to you and me.

If you happen to be a "high roller" who plays exclusively with $25 and $100 chips, free accommodations, free food, free shows, free girls, even free transportation to and from Nevada and while you're there — they are all yours, usually without asking.

Even if you play with $1 or $5 chips, "comps" for meals and shows are often available, as are your room accommodations at what are called "casino rates." These rates usually are well below the going rates at the hotel's check-in desk. At all major hotels blocks of rooms are allotted to their casino managers who dispose of them as they please to "deserving" customers. When the room clerk tells you that he's booked solid, go play a little $5 or $10 craps or blackjack, and then after a bit, tackle the pit boss. More often than not, he'll take care of you.

In any case, casino gambling keeps growing in popularity, and the bastions of those who would deny us the privilege of doing as we please with our own money are beginning to crumble. They will continue to crumble for one very potent reason. Gambling is a great and largely untapped source of tax revenues, and our politicians' hunger for taxes is absolutely insatiable.

Within the past few years a half-dozen states have instituted state lotteries; New Jersey has legalized casino gambling, and initiatives toward that same end are being promoted and planned in another half-dozen states including California and Florida. Perhaps 15 or 20 states have horse and dog racing, and so on.

A truly ridiculous aspect of the restrictions we allow politicians to impose on us is the fact that the legalized racing and lotteries endorsed and promoted by them are absolutely larcenous as compared with the major casino games. Those pious expressions of concern for the public welfare that we hear so often in this connection are pure unadulterated hypocrisy.

In California, where I live, the pari-mutuels and the state take 17 percent or 18 percent "off the top" before the horseplayers get paid. I believe the average "take" of the state lotteries is something like 40 percent off the top. California, of course, contributes an enormous share of the gaming revenues that keep Nevada so healthy and prosperous despite its low taxes. Meanwhile, our own sales taxes, state income tax, property taxes, inventory taxes, etc., stunt the growth of our economy and erode the vitality, self-sufficiency, and incentives of our people.

To me there are few things quite as abhorrent as the sanctimonious mouthings of politicians about our "blessed freedoms," while at every level of government they hack away at those freedoms one by one.

My personal views and comments might be somewhat more charitable were it not for the fact that while they debase our currency, squandering the public's money in myriad ways over which the public has absolutely no control, these same politicians never miss a chance to add to their own swollen emoluments, their perquisites, and of course, their retirement benefits — usually without even recording their votes on such matters. Thus, they avoid being held to personal account for their actions.

As this is written I am told that half the population of the United States — not to mention other parts of the world — is now directly or indirectly supported by the other half. The once almighty dollar is nosediving in the world's marketplaces, while our productive, inventive and commercial genius is being progressively stifled by government meddling and regulation.

So be of good cheer; we are headed for a cataclysm which, when it comes, will make the "Boston Tea Party" look like a tea party indeed. Maybe, when that day arrives, casino gambling will have become this country's major industry. After all,

1974, which was a recession year for most of the country and almost all industries, turned out to be a record-breaking boom year for Las Vegas.

I pray that I may be forgiven for diverting slightly into the murky field of politics and away from the real theme of this book. Perhaps in the recesses of my mind there has always lurked a suspicion that gambling interests and political interests were mysteriously but inextricably linked together.

Be that as it may, dear reader, I hope most sincerely that within these pages you will have found something of value; something that will prove to benefit where it counts most, whenever you venture into the exciting world of casino craps, blackjack, roulette, and high rollers.

THE END